Sew Home

FEB 2017

Learn Design Basics, Techniques, Fabrics & Supplies

30+ Modern Projects to Turn a House into YOUR Home

Erin Schlosser

stash BOOKS®
an imprint of C&T Publishing

Text copyright © 2016 by Erin Schlosser

Photography and artwork copyright © 2016 by C&T Publishing, Inc.

Publisher: Amy Marson

Creative Director: Gailen Runge

Editors: Liz Aneloski and Karla Menaugh

Technical Editors: Julie Waldman and Debbie Rodgers

Cover/Book Designer: April Mostek

Production Coordinators: Freesia Pearson Blizard and Tim Manibusan

Production Editors: Alice Mace Nakanishi, Jennifer Warren, and Nicole Rolandelli

Illustrator: Tim Manibusan

Photo Assistant: Carly Jean Marin

Style photography by Page + Pixel, Lucy Glover, and Carly Jean Marin and instructional photography by Diane Pedersen, unless otherwise noted

Published by Stash Books, an imprint of C&T Publishing, Inc., P.O. Box 1456, Lafayette, CA 94549

Library of Congress Cataloging-in-Publication Data

Names: Schlosser, Erin, 1982- author.

Title: Sew home : learn design basics, techniques, fabrics & supplies--30+ modern projects to turn a house into your home / Erin Schlosser.

Description: Lafayette, CA : C&T Publishing, Inc., [2016] | Includes bibliographical references.

Identifiers: LCCN 2015049120 | ISBN 9781617451584 (soft cover)

Subjects: LCSH: House furnishings. | Sewing.

Classification: LCC TT387 .S35 2016 | DDC 646.2/1--dc23

LC record available at http://lccn.loc.gov/2015049120

Printed in China

10 9 8 7 6 5 4 3 2 1

Dedication

This book is dedicated to all the makers, designers, doers, sewists, and DIYers out there. Go big, go bold, and listen to yourself when designing your space. After all, you're the one who's living there!

Acknowledgments

I want to thank my family for their never-ending support of my creative pursuits. Thanks to my dad and mom, from whom I got a perfect blend of work ethic, go-get-'em attitude, and creativity; to my brother and sister, who provided inspiration and technical support; and most especially to my husband, whose gourmet cooking, endless support, and pep talks kept me going.

Thank you to everyone at C&T Publishing for making my dream a reality.

Contents

Project
Skill Levels

1: Beginner

2: Confident Beginner

3: Intermediate

4: Advanced

Introduction

From the first "quillow" my grandmother helped me make, my love of functional sewing projects was born. Ever since then, I have loved sharing and discussing tips, techniques, and tricks with eager sewists. When I bought my first home, I made a list of all the custom household items I wanted to design and create, and the various sewing techniques that would be necessary. This became the genesis for this book and the projects you will discover here. Within these pages you'll find inspirational projects for a variety of skill levels and for every room in your home—whatever your style.

If you're not in the mood to pull out the sewing machine, you can make fun projects that don't require one, such as the Cornice Board (page 40) or the DIY Rug (page 110). If you don't have a lot of time but want to create something quick to impress your guests, try the Customized Sheets (page 54) or Rolled-Hem Napkins (page 83). If you're new to sewing, start out with one of my basic projects like Fancy Flange Shams (page 57) or the Quick and Easy Tablecloth (page 75). Soon enough you'll be making lined and pleated Drapes (page 43) or a Corded Throw Pillow (page 113).

Together we'll cover the theory of design and how to choose a style that works for you. We'll master the arts of installing invisible zippers, lining drapes, making custom lighting, and so much more. As you learn and are inspired, you'll be able to transform your dwelling into a space that reflects your personality, your imagination, and your dreams.

1

Principles and Elements of Design

Choosing fabrics for home-sewing projects doesn't have to be stressful. With a few basic tips and some knowledge of the foundations of design, you'll be armed with what you need to make good design choices.

When working on sewing projects for the home, it's important to keep in mind that you may already have a sense of how you want the space to feel and a grasp of basic design theory. In this case, go with what makes you happy! If you're not familiar with the principles and elements, let me give you a quick introduction.

The principles and elements work together to provide a visually pleasing space. In a way, the principles of design are the theory behind how to use the more concrete elements of design. You'd plan a space using theory and apply the elements to accomplish your design. It's kind of like cooking: you can have all the ingredients, but unless you know how to prep those ingredients and in what quantities to use them, the recipe won't turn out very well. Here's an introduction to the elements and principles of design.

Elements of Design

This gorgeous tile floor illustrates a pattern, one of the elements of design.

Space (positive and negative): Patterns and designs can be made from both positive and negative space—that is, the space that is your subject and the space that is not your subject.

Shape: The two-dimensional outline of a geometric figure (such as a circle or hexagon) or an organic form.

Form: The three-dimensional shape of an object, such as a vase or chair.

Visual mass: The visual size or weight of an object. For example, a small bright red vase can have more visual mass than a larger white vase. The red coloring makes it feel more visually heavy.

Line: Any type of connection between points. The connection can be curvilinear, straight, or zigzag. It can be implied or actual. The alignment of furniture can make a line, just as a striped fabric has lines.

Texture: Any natural or implied surface pattern. Texture can easily add warmth to a space.

Pattern: Motifs or other elements arranged in an ordered way.

Light (natural or artificial): Light can impact how other elements and principles are interpreted by the eye.

Color: Hues and values seen by the eye.

Principles of Design

Scale: The size of an object.

Proportion: How elements relate to each other and the space around them in size. Keeping fabric and other design elements in proportion to the space is important. A super-sized pattern can seem out of place in a small space.

Balance: Elements can be balanced symmetrically, asymmetrically, or radially (in a circle). You can achieve balance with pillows on a sofa or with a balance of color. Use the elements to provide balance.

Rhythm: The way repeating elements give movement to a space. They keep your eye moving. Rhythm can be boring unless emphasis and variety are added.

Emphasis: The coordination of elements to form a focal point. This can be done using space, light, color, or any of the other elements of design.

Harmony: How elements work with one another to provide a well-designed space.

Variety: Breaking up the rhythm using a combination of line, color, or other elements. Variety keeps things interesting.

Finding Inspiration

You've probably heard it before, but inspiration is everywhere! If you're feeling stumped about what to do for a room design, go for a walk around your neighborhood, favorite park, downtown—anywhere that inspires you and makes you happy. Take a series of photos of objects that you like. Your photos could show an overall scene, like a main street, or extreme close-ups of a natural or architectural feature that spoke to you. Many times inspiration will strike from the most unlikely of sources.

Both man-made and natural elements can be a source of inspiration.

You can use your inspiration photos in a variety of ways. You can transfer color palettes, fabric patterns, and design elements to your interior space.

When selecting a color palette, remember to include different values of the color.

I loved the stonework pattern in the photo, and this inspired my main fabric choice.

The small motif in this stonework inspired my floor cushion.

Mixing and Matching Prints

The easiest route for choosing coordinating prints is to find one line of fabric and use all of its coordinates in the space. However, while easy, this option often results in a room that's more matchy-matchy than a beautifully designed space. This is where the elements and principles of design come into play.

I typically start with one color of fabric or one print I really love. Then I try to mix up the value and scale to find appropriate coordinates. I also try to find a blend of organic and geometric prints. Keep in mind that many small-scale fabrics will actually appear as a solid color from a distance. Although you look at fabrics from an arm's length away while shopping, you usually view most interior fabrics from a greater distance. If you're not sure whether a fabric you select will read as a solid, pin it to the wall in the intended space, then step back and see if it looks the way you expected.

When you are laying out and choosing your fabrics, display them in proportions similar to how they will be used. The main fabric should be the largest piece, while coordinating prints should be viewed in smaller swatches. This keeps everything in proportion so you can more accurately determine how they will look in the space.

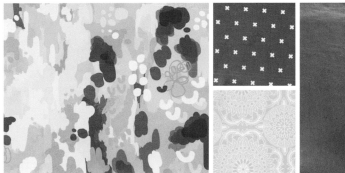

Whether you are working with just a few fabrics or an entire room, display fabrics proportionally to visualize them more easily.

Many stores will give you a small sample swatch. While the swatch can help with color coordination, it's difficult to see the full pattern on such a small piece of fabric. Take a quick photo of the bolt so you can remember what the full pattern looks like. Also take a photo of its information tag so you can remember the store, item number, and price.

My Personal Design Philosophy

There is rarely ever one right way to design a space. Even when I work with my clients, I typically choose two great options and then ask them to select the one they prefer. Once you have a grasp of the basic elements and principles of design, you have the parameters from which you can break the rules.

Also don't forget that it's easy to personalize any of the projects! Choose a favorite trip photo and have a company print it on fabric. Then you have the material to make an accent pillow or to complete the storage bins, the clock, or any number of projects in the book.

In the end, choose what you like, what's comfortable to you, and what works for the scale of the space—and own it!

2
Home Decor Fabric Basics

Choosing Fabrics and Determining Yardage

Home Decor Fabrics

You've probably noticed that home decor fabric is a bit different from apparel fabric or quilting-weight cottons. Home decor fabric is usually rolled on a tube instead of folded and can range in width from 54″ to 60″. The pattern typically has a larger scale that is more suitable for the interior of a home, and the fabric is thicker and more durable. The price can range from about $12 per yard all the way to $200 or more per yard.

Myriad fabric options are available for home decor sewing. Here are a majority of the more popular ones, their description, how they drape, and their typical uses.

Jacquard: This type of fabric has a design that's woven into the fabric. It is typically a heavier weight and is used for upholstery and drapery.

Print: This fabric comes in a variety of substrates (cotton, polyester, and so on) and has a pattern printed directly onto the fabric. Depending on the base fabric, prints can be used for just about anything!

Tip • If you fall in love with an expensive fabric and just have to have it, keep this in mind:

If you bought ½ yard for $100 and made 2 pillow fronts, you would be paying almost the same as if you bought a premade pillow from a high-end design store. Using an expensive fabric in small amounts can have a big impact too!

Silk: Silk is a natural fabric that has a sheen and drapes beautifully. It is typically used for window treatments.

Twill-Medium: A heavy-weight woven fabric used for upholstery. Twill-medium works well for upholstery because it wears well.

Leather/Faux Leather: Natural and man-made leather look-alikes work great for upholstery and pillows.

Fabrics, from left to right: jacquard, print, silk, faux leather

Note: The fabric from this book came from a variety of sources. I obtained most of the fabric from the following:

Candy Kirby Designs
Dear Stella Fabrics
FreeSpirit Fabrics
High Fashion Home
Karen Lewis Textiles
Sew Caroline—*Happy Home* fabric printed by Art Gallery Fabrics
Windham Fabrics

Keep in mind that unconventional premade products can also provide yardage for projects. If you find a favorite fabric but it's already a shower curtain, drape, or tablecloth, no one is saying it has to stay that way! Cut it up to make place mats, pillows, or a lamp shade cover.

The first step to many home decor projects, such as window coverings, is to measure the area where you will use the project. Once you have used your measurements to determine the cutting size of the project piece, you will need to figure out the correct yardage to purchase. Then it is time to buy fabric.

Railroaded Fabric

You may have heard the term *railroaded fabric* before, but what does that mean? It simply means that the design is oriented parallel to the selvage, rather than from selvage to selvage.

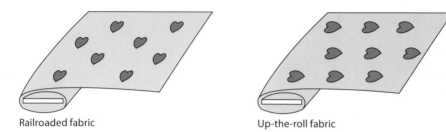

Railroaded fabric   Up-the-roll fabric

Why is this important? Say you want to use a large-scale horizontal stripe for window treatments. If the stripe is railroaded, the drape will end up with vertical stripes instead of the horizontal stripes you were planning. Keep in mind how the fabric will be cut before you purchase it; otherwise you may be in for a costly surprise.

Railroaded fabric on a drapery panel   Up-the-roll fabric on a drapery panel

Railroaded fabric can be handy when making a headboard or cornice board. These projects are typically much more wide than tall, so using a railroaded pattern will mean that no piecing is necessary to get the width you need. Just buy enough yardage for the width plus a bit extra for seams or wrapping around the headboard or cornice board.

Working with Fabric Pattern Repeats

The repeat refers to the width and length of fabric before the pattern repeats itself. For most projects, you will need to note the size of both the vertical and horizontal repeat. In some cases, the size of the repeat may be listed on the tag as part of the fabric information. If not, you can find it using a ruler or tape measure. Start at one point in the pattern, and move horizontally until that same part of the pattern repeats itself. Measure that distance. This will be the horizontal repeat. Do the same for a vertical element within the pattern to find the vertical repeat.

If you plan to cut multiple drapes from the same fabric, always add in one extra repeat for each piece that needs to be cut.

For example, if I need 3 yards per window panel and I need to make 4 panels, I'd need (3 yards + my repeat) × 4. If my repeat were 16″, I'd need to purchase 3 yards plus 16″ per panel, and multiply that times 4 to have enough material to make my 4 panels.

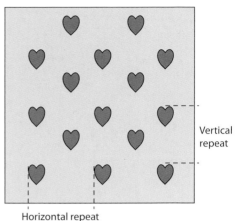

Vertical repeat

Horizontal repeat

Finding the repeat

Determining Yardage

After you have determined the size and orientation of the repeats, you're ready to do a little math. If it's easier for you to visualize, draw a simple diagram. Say you need to sew together a rectangle that's 70″ × 80″. Draw a rectangle 70″ × 80″, then draw a width of fabric that covers this amount. Continue drawing in widths, taking into account the fabric width, until you've covered the shape. To see how much fabric to purchase, add up how many pieces of fabric you need.

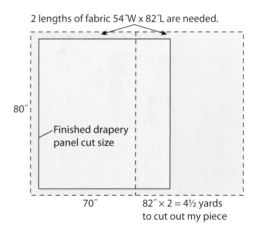

2 lengths of fabric 54″W x 82″L are needed.

80″

Finished drapery panel cut size

70″

82″ x 2 = 4½ yards to cut out my piece

Remember not to count the selvages in the width. I usually plan on using a couple of inches less than the full fabric width for a safe estimate.

Cutting Techniques

Cutting Fabric with Large Repeats

Cutting decor fabric correctly is essential to the look of the finished product. If you need to cut a straight line, always cut it parallel to the selvage of the fabric. Trim off the selvage itself. During the manufacturing process, the selvage is woven in a slightly different, tighter weave than the main fabric. If you do not trim it, the difference in weave can distort seams in your finished product.

What if the beautiful fabric you choose has a large-scale repeat? Don't let this scare you off, but buy enough extra fabric so you can match up the repeat in all the seams. It's important in a space that has multiples of the same window treatment or pillow that the repeats all match. If you simply cut out 3 full-length drapes from a 10-yard length of fabric, you may end up with 1 or more panels with a misaligned pattern.

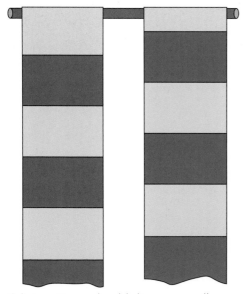

Fabric patterns *should* align across all window treatments in the same space.

The easy solution is to first cut out just 1 piece of fabric for your project. Use a fabric-marking tool to mark the center of the main pattern in your fabric. From that point, measure half of the cut size of your project piece both vertically and horizontally, and make additional markings. Then cut the piece that you need for the Roman shade, drape, pillow, or other project.

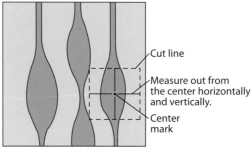

Cut line

Measure out from the center horizontally and vertically.

Center mark

If I needed a 24″ square with a pattern centered, I'd find the center, then mark 12″ from either side and make the cut lines.

Now place the cut piece directly on top of the fabric, lining up the fabric pattern of the cut piece with the remaining fabric. Use this piece as the template to cut out the other pieces in the set.

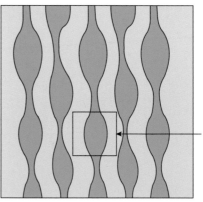

A centered and cut piece, placed and used as a pattern

Cutting multiple pieces with the same repeat

How to Cut Large Pieces of Fabric in a Limited Space

Professional drapery workrooms can have huge spaces in which to lay out the wide fabric and cut. Most of us sewing at home don't have that amount of space to spare. I cut out all my window treatments and other projects on a table with only a 24″ × 36″ cutting mat. A few extra tools are necessary to make this work: a new, sharp rotary blade in the rotary cutter and a large cutting ruler with a lip on one short edge.

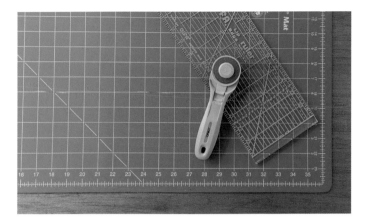

The ruler with a lip works very similar to how a T-square works to get a nice 90° cut. Line up the fabric selvage along a straight horizontal line on the cutting mat. Set the ruler on the cutting mat with the lip pressed against the cutting mat edge. Line up the ruler on the vertical line you're cutting, press down, and use the rotary cutter along the ruler edge to cut a straight line.

To cut a piece wider than the cutting mat, carefully fold the fabric so that the fold and selvage line up, then pin the fabric in place. Now use the ruler and cutting mat to cut correctly. Since you may be cutting through four thick layers, using a new, sharp rotary blade is ideal.

Note: Consider using the larger 60mm rotary cutter to more easily cut through thick layers.

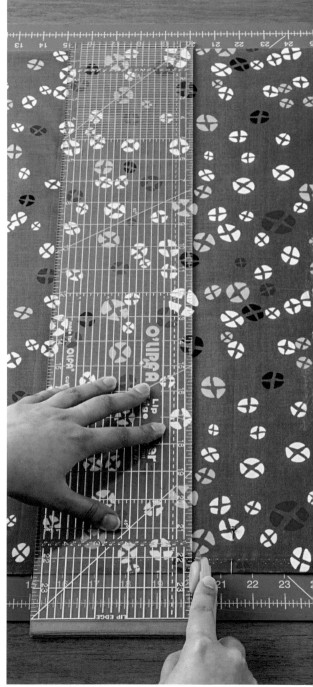

Try to make one clean cut. Start close to you, press down firmly, and cut away with one clear motion.

Getting Ready to Sew with Home Decor Fabric

Choosing Thread

When sewing with home decor fabric, I use a polyester or poly/cotton blend thread in a coordinating color. Quilting weight fabrics can be sewn with 100% cotton thread if desired.

If I need to use a clear monofilament thread, I invest in a high-quality thread.

Note: Do your research, because your sewing machine manufacturer may have a preferred monofilament thread.

Monofilament thread typically comes in smoke and clear colors.

When sewing with monofilament thread, consider using a vertical spool pin to help the thread unwind neatly. Be sure to test the thread on a scrap of fabric to get your machine's tension settings correct. Because the monofilament thread is so fine, I typically use a size 70/10 universal needle or microtex needle.

Note: I use the following threads:
- Aurifil cotton thread
- Mettler polyester thread
- Coats & Clark Outdoor thread
- YLI Wonder Invisible Thread

Choosing a Sewing Needle

The right sewing needle can affect how professional your project looks. Unfortunately, no one needle is right for all home decor sewing. The following table shows a few different sizes and types of needles that work well for me.

Most needle types come in a variety of sizes. The larger the number, the larger the needle, and the thicker the fabric you can sew with it.

Universal: These needles have a slightly rounded point and are great general needles for most sewing projects.

Microtex: These needles have a very fine point that will keep lightweight fabrics from pulling, puckering, and snagging.

Leather Needle: These needles have a point that cuts through the leather or vinyl as it stitches, making a clean path for the thread.

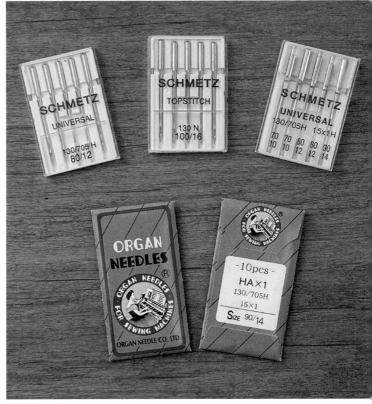

Just a few of my favorite needles

Choosing a Sewing Needle

Needle Size	Fabric Weight	Fabric Types
60/8, 65/9	Extremely lightweight	Silk, organza, sheer fabrics
70/10, 75/11	Lightweight	Voile, fine lace, gauze, microfiber
80/12, 90/14	Medium weight	Cotton, linen, poplin, satin, brocade
100/16, 110/18	Heavyweight	Denim, tweed, canvas, leather/pleather, upholstery-weight woven fabric

Basic Home Decor Sewing Techniques

Basting Stitch

A basting stitch is a long stitch designed to temporarily hold pieces in place. Remove it after you have completed the project.

Glue Basting

To glue baste, use a washable glue and a small glue tip to glue the fabric in place; then heat set the glue. You can glue baste instead of using a basting stitch.

Edge Stitch

The edge stitch is a straight line sewn right along the edge of the fabric, ⅛″ or less away from the edge. I use this stitch often in double-fold hems (next page) or to close turned openings.

Cording

With the right sewing machine foot, making custom cording is easy! Cording will take any pillow or cushion from blah to beautiful.

STEP 1

Cut a bias strip at 45° to the selvage. **FIGURE A**

The width of the bias strip will depend on the diameter of the cording. A strip cut to the proper width will be able to fully enclose the cord and provide approximately a ½″ seam allowance on the top and bottom. Use a tape measure to measure around the cord and add 1″ to ensure you have the proper seam allowance.

STEP 2

To complete the cording, wrap the cord inside the bias strip. Using a cording foot and a basting stitch, sew directly along the edge of the wrapped cord. If the cord is larger than the opening in the cording foot, use a narrow zipper foot instead and move the needle position to stitch directly next to the cord. **FIGURE B**

Leave both ends open a few inches for completing the cording later.

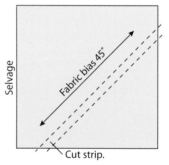

A Cutting on the bias gives fabric a nice stretch, which makes turning corners with cording easier and keeps folded fabric from puckering.

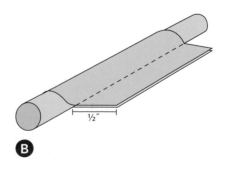

STEP 3

To attach the cording to a pillow, cushion, or other project, line up the raw edges of the cording with the raw outer edge of the main fabric. Baste in place, still using the cording foot or zipper foot. When you turn the corners, clip the seam allowance a bit to ease the turn; just don't clip past the basting stitch. **FIGURE C**

STEP 4

Leave both ends unstitched a few inches. At the beginning end of the cording, move the cord to the side, unfold the bias strip a few inches along the length, and fold the end under ½″, wrong sides together. Trim the cord to 1″ shorter than the folded end. Now place the other end of the wrapped cording inside the folded section. Trim any extra bias fabric past about 2″–3″. Trim the cord so the end butts up against the beginning end. Encase the cording again, pin, and complete stitching the cording. **FIGURE D**

Double-Fold Hem

Make a double-fold hem by folding up the raw edge to the width listed in the instructions, then folding the hem up again to enclose the raw edge. For example, a 2″ double-fold hem would be folded up a scant 2″, then another 2″ to enclose the edge. Most often, you will finish the hem with an edge stitch (previous page) or a blind hem (page 24).

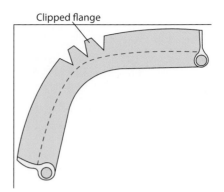

Clipped flange

C Round the cording around the pillow corner.

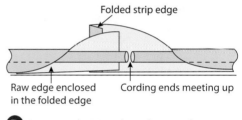

Folded strip edge

Raw edge enclosed in the folded edge

Cording ends meeting up

D A correctly joined cording end

Blind Hem

With the correct presser foot, sewing a blind hem is easy and gives a gorgeous, professional finish to your custom home sewing projects.

Folding and pressing a hem to prepare it for the blind stitch is no different from folding and pressing any other hem. The difference is in how it is stitched.

STEP 1

Fold the raw edge of the hem up, then fold it again and press well. **FIGURE A**

STEP 2

From the wrong side of the fabric, fold the hem up, right sides together, and leave the first fold hanging over the soft fold about ¼″–⅜″. Pin as often as needed, but *don't* press this fold—a pressed crease line will emphasize the place where your blind hem is located. After you sew the blind hem, you will unfold this fold and press well. The blind hem will disappear into the fabric. **FIGURE B**

STEP 3

Attach the blind hem foot to the machine and use the blind stitch setting.

Tip • The blind stitch should look similar to this.

STEP 4

Place the fold of the fabric up against the flange on the blind hem foot. Stitch with the majority of the stitching line on the ¼″–⅜″ overhanging fold, with the left side of the stitch barely catching the folded hem. **FIGURE C**

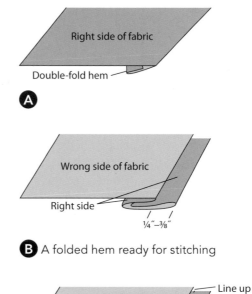

Right side of fabric

Double-fold hem

A

Wrong side of fabric

Right side

¼″–⅜″

B A folded hem ready for stitching

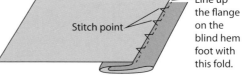

Line up the flange on the blind hem foot with this fold.

Stitch point

C The stitch point will just barely catch the folded section.

Standard Zipper

Many different methods can be used to attach a standard zipper. This method adds a flange to conceal a regular zipper.

STEP 1

Using a ½″ seam and a basting stitch, stitch together the 2 edges of fabric where the zipper will be located. Press the seam open.

STEP 2

Place the zipper behind the pressed open seam with the zipper teeth touching the back of the seam. Center the teeth on the seam. Pin the zipper in place, or glue baste it with a fine-tip point. **FIGURE D**

STEP 3

From the right side of the fabric (the zipper will be hidden), stitch down both sides of the basted seam, ¼″ from the seam. If needed, use a zipper foot to get close to the zipper teeth hidden under the fabric. Take out the basting stitches to reveal the zipper. Open the zipper partway, pulling the zipper pull through one short, unstitched edge. Stitch across each short end of the zipper to complete the zipper installation. **FIGURE E**

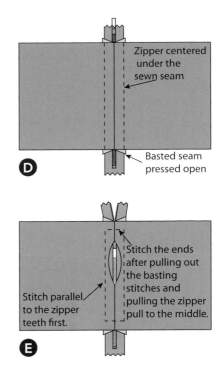

Zipper centered under the sewn seam

Basted seam pressed open

D

Stitch the ends after pulling out the basting stitches and pulling the zipper pull to the middle.

Stitch parallel to the zipper teeth first.

E

Concealed Zipper

A concealed zipper is best sewn with a concealed zipper foot. This type of zipper is practically invisible when sewn correctly.

STEP 1

Place the project pieces right sides together with the edge for the invisible zipper facing you. Place the zipper on top. At both ends of the zipper, place a small mark across the edges of both fabric pieces and the width of the zipper. These marks will be the stopping and starting points for stitching, as well as the alignment points for all the pieces. **FIGURE F**

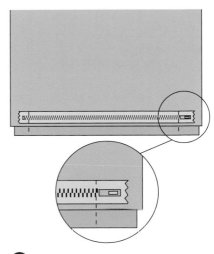

F Each end will have 4 marks: 2 on the fabric and 2 on the zipper.

STEP 2

Place the right side of the zipper (the side with the zipper pull) facedown on the right side of the fabric. Align the noncoiled edge of the zipper with the raw edge of the fabric, matching the alignment marks from Step 1. Pin (or glue baste) the zipper in place. **FIGURE G**

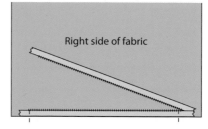

G Align the noncoiled edge of the zipper with the raw edge of the fabric.

STEP 3

Attach the concealed zipper foot to your sewing machine. Place the coil of the zipper directly under the left groove of the foot. Start at a marked point and stitch to the opposite point, backstitching at the starting and stopping points. **FIGURE H**

STEP 4

Place the other fabric piece right side down on top of the first piece. Fold the edge back slightly. Pull up the unsewn side of the zipper and match up the noncoiled edge with the raw edge of the fabric. Align the marked points on the zipper and fabric. The right side of the zipper should still be facing the right side of the fabric. Pin (or glue baste) in place. **FIGURE I**

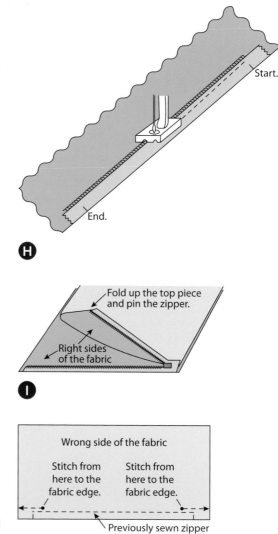

H

I

STEP 5

Place the coil of the zipper under the left groove of the zipper foot and stitch from one marked point to the other, backstitching at each end.

STEP 6

To complete both ends and finish the seam, unzip the zipper halfway, and then refold the fabrics, right sides together. Switch to a regular zipper foot for this step. Place the project under the zipper foot and position the needle so that you sew as close to the zipper teeth as possible. Start ¼″ inside each mark, backstitch, and continue sewing to the edge of the seam to complete the concealed zipper. **FIGURE J**

J Offset the stitch slightly so you don't sew directly on the zipper teeth.

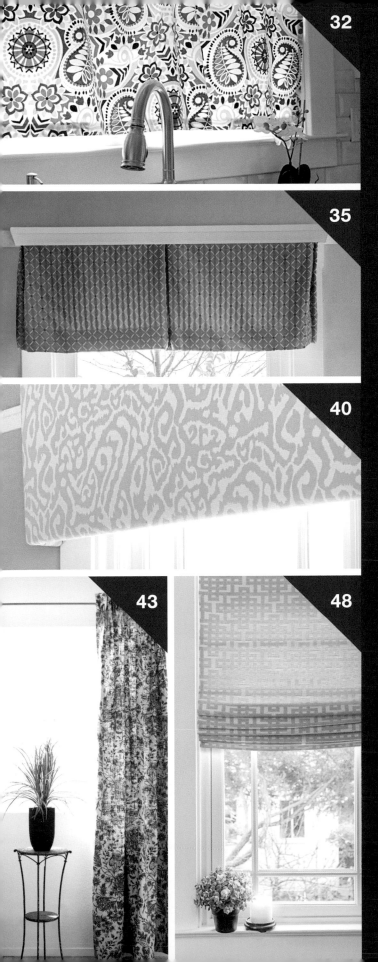

3

Window Treatments

What Style Should I Choose?

Choosing the right type of window treatment doesn't have to be difficult. Asking yourself a few simple questions to help with the process of selecting the appropriate window treatment design for your space is the easiest way to get started.

Question 1

What type of feel do I want for the space?

Is the room going to have a more casual, lived-in feel or be a dressy dining room? Are the windows in a media room or an elegant master bedroom? These questions will determine the style of the window treatment. Straight rod-pocket panels are more casual, while pleated panels have a dressier feel.

Question 2

Will the window treatment be functional or decorative?

Will it be closed every night or stay open while blinds or shutters provide privacy?

The answer to this question will determine how much fabric is needed and how many panels need to be made. For example, functional drapes for three large windows will require enough fabric to close the drapes across all three windows and still have some fullness. Decorative drapes for the same windows would require only enough fabric to make two narrow panels that are always pulled to the side.

Question 3

Do the windows receive direct sunlight, or are they on a side of the home that is mostly shaded?

South-facing windows typically receive the most direct sun, while north-facing windows usually are shaded. You would need different types of lining for sunny and shady windows.

After you answer these questions, it will be easier to choose a design for the space. If you need some ideas, search inspirational sites online like Pinterest or Houzz, as well as the plethora of design magazines.

Not sure if a window treatment is casual or more dressy? Analyze the inspiration photos you've chosen. Is the window treatment you are considering used in a casual game room, or a formal dining room? This may give you some clues on whether it's appropriate for your space. However, don't let that be a make-or-break rule. If you are a more casual dining person, use casual, relaxed drapes in the formal dining room. Always do what feels comfortable for you—after all, it's your home!

How Do You Visualize Potential Designs?

Sometimes it's hard to visualize how a certain window treatment will look in your own space. To test designs, I use the following trick:

STEP 1

Take a photo or two of the space where you will hang your window treatments. Include some of the floor and ceiling in the room photo, not just the windows. This allows you to sketch scaled designs more easily. If you don't include the floor and ceiling, it's much more difficult to judge the scale, size, and position of the window treatments. I also try to draw the ceiling and wall lines to help see the design better. (This is a great cheater way to draw a room perspective also!)

The correct photo includes the floor, ceiling, and other walls.

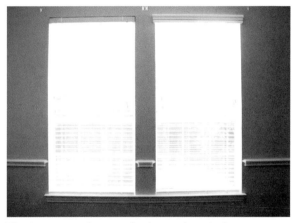

The incorrect photo only shows the windows.

STEP 2

Print these photos on standard paper. (No need to get them professionally printed on photo paper; regular copy paper from a home printer will be fine.) Cut some thin tracing paper to the size of the photo. Place the tracing paper over the photo and use washi tape to hold it in place.

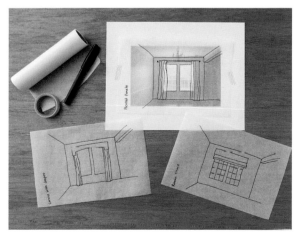

STEP 3

Now quickly sketch one of the designs from your inspiration images. Remove the first tracing paper sheet and add another one to the photo. Sketch a different window treatment. Repeat for all the designs you're considering. This process will help you see what you like and will reveal any that don't quite look right in the space.

Tips

• *Always design full-length drapes long enough to hang just below the ceiling line or crown molding. This will help add visual height to the windows and room.*

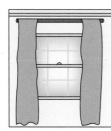 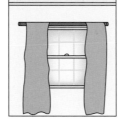

Right way   Wrong way

• *Hang drapes to the side of the window, so the fabric is just slightly overlapping the window edge. This will make the windows appear much larger.*

 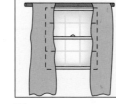

Right way   Wrong way

• *Remember, window treatments are often paired. Roman shades might be paired with panels, or panels might be paired and layered under a cornice board.*

Sometimes, you may have two options that are equally good for the space. Choose one that you love and go for it!

Lining Basics

The many different types of window linings serve a variety of purposes that are both functional and decorative. Use the same color of lining for the entire home. Typically, the linings will be either white or ivory. Using a lining provides a pleasing view of your windows from the exterior of the home. Imagine choosing five different fabrics for the various rooms of the home, sewing the window treatments, then going outside and looking at your home. Without the linings, you would see a different fabric in each window.

Lining will protect the more expensive decorator fabric from the effects of the sun, such as color fading and deterioration. Lining can also preserve the design of the fabric. Without a lining to filter the sun, the print and colors of the main fabric can look washed out.

Lining widths vary from 40″ to 120″. The fabrics typically are a blend of cotton and polyester for durability and stability. It's best to buy fabric that covers the width of the window treatment instead of piecing two smaller widths together.

Some standard types of lining include basic lining, blackout lining, and thermal lining.

Shown are a basic lining and a blackout lining. The basic lining will feel very similar to a light- to mid-weight cotton, while the blackout lining typically has a rubbery finish on the back.

Lining can really change how the curtain looks in the window. Shown here are two identical curtains, one with a lining and one without.

Basic Lining: Use a basic lining for most projects. Basic lining is lightweight and can be used with thin and thick materials.

Blackout Lining: This lining type has a barrier that blocks out light. Use blackout lining where the drapes are functional and a minimal amount of light is desired. A baby's room, media room, or master bedroom would be good places for blackout lining.

Thermal Lining: Use thermal lining on functional drapes if you are in a particularly hot or cold climate. This type of lining will assist in keeping out heat or cold and maintaining a more comfortable temperature in the space.

Drapery Hardware

Drapery hardware also can have different styles. Traditional hardware can be a fluted rod with ornate finials. More contemporary hardware can be made from metal and acrylic.

Once you've chosen a drapery style, choose a similar style of hardware for a polished look.

Remember to pay attention to the scale of the room, drapes, and hardware as well. Full-length pleated panels in a room with a high ceiling will need larger-diameter hardware than a small café curtain hanging in a kitchen window.

Tip • Refer to Chapter 2 (page 13) for a reminder on how to cut and piece fabric repeats.

Now that we have covered the basics of window treatments, it's time to sew!

Café Curtain

FINISHED SIZE: Custom

Materials and Supplies

- Light/medium-weight home decor fabric
- Blind hem presser foot for your sewing machine
- Tension rod to fit window, ⅝″ or smaller diameter

Measuring and Cutting

STEP 1

Measure the window width inside the frame and determine how long you want the finished café curtain to be. Typically, these curtains cover ½ to ⅓ of the window height.

_____ Window width

_____ Desired curtain length

Now for the math to determine the piece that will need to be cut:

Window width _____ × 1.5 = _____ + 2″ = _____ curtain cut width

Desired curtain length _____ + 3¼″ = _____ curtain cut length

For example, if I had a 36″-wide window and I wanted my café curtain to be 15″ long, I'd use these 2 measurements to place in the equation above.

(36″ × 1.5) + 2 = 56″ and 15″ + 3¼″ = 18¼″

In this example, the piece I would need to cut would be 56″ × 18¼″. Enter the measurements you took and determine the final size of your cut piece. Refer to Working with Fabric Pattern Repeats and Determining Yardage (page 17) to determine how much fabric you need and how to match up and piece repeats as needed.

STEP 2

Cut out the curtain from the measurements above, making sure you've trimmed off the selvages first.

Café curtains are great for a little privacy in a breakfast nook or kitchen window. Use a fun kitschy print or a classic geometric pattern and get sewing! Café curtains also work well to cover open shelves and vanity openings when you want to hide a bit of clutter.

Techniques Learned/Practiced

- Sewing a blind hem

Construction

STEP 1

Carefully press each side in ½˝ and make a double fold to fully enclose the raw edge. Edgestitch (page 22) each folded edge.

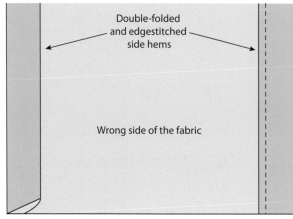

Finish the side seams.

Tip • Always test the iron setting on a small scrap to make sure that the fabric won't burn, melt, or distort with heat.

STEP 2

Press the bottom edge under ½˝, then fold 1˝ to enclose the raw edge. Finish with a blind hem (page 24). Press well.

STEP 3

To make the rod pocket, fold the top edge ¼˝ and press well. Fold again 1½˝ and press. Finish the folded edge with an edge stitch (page 22).

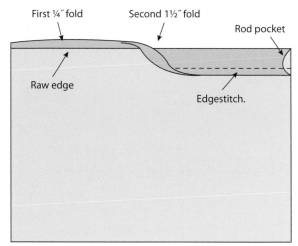

Complete the rod pocket.

STEP 4

Slide the tension rod into the curtain and hang.

Tips

• *Add some pom-poms or other decorative trim for a bit of fun.*

• *If the curtain will be near a dining table or kitchen sink, consider using a water repellent like Scotchgard to keep it in pristine condition.*

Inverted Pleat Valance

FINISHED SIZE: Custom

A pleated valance doesn't have to be stuffy. With crisply pressed pleats and a modern fabric, you can have a sharp window treatment in no time. These look great on their own but can also be combined with roman shades or full-length panels.

Techniques Learned/Practiced

- **Making pleats**
- **Working with lining**
- **Mitering drape corners**

Materials and Supplies

- Any home decor or quilting-weight cotton (Determine the yardage by the window size. See Measuring and Cutting, Step 1, below.)
- Lining fabric
- 1″ × 4″ wooden board
- Saw
- 3–5 L-brackets, 3″ wide
- Screws and screwdriver

Tip • Remember that wood at the home improvement store is in nominal sizing. This means that a 1″ × 4″ board is actually a bit smaller than 1″ × 4″.

Measuring and Cutting

STEP 1

Measure the width of the window opening.

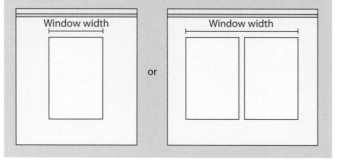

Note: You could use the valance on 1 larger window or 2 smaller windows placed side by side. Either way, measure across the entire width.

Window width + 6″ = _____ board cut length

Window width + 13″ = _____ finished valance width

Next, add enough width for the side seams and pleats.

Tip • For a more modern and contemporary feel, I like to limit my pleats to one in the middle and one on each corner.

Add 28″ to the finished valance width measurement above. This adds 8″ for each of the 3 pleats and 2″ for each of the side hems.

Finished valance width + 28″ = _____ valance cut width

For example, if I were making a valance for a 36″ window:

Window width (36″) + 6″ = 42″ board cut length

Window width (36″) + 13″ = 49″ finished valance width

Finished valance width (49″) + 28″ = 77″ valance cut width

A standard valance height for a window in a room with an 8′–10′ ceiling is 15″. If you have taller ceilings and larger windows, use an 18″ height for proper scale.

Add 8″ to the finished valance height for hems and the top.

Finished valance height + 8″ = _____ valance cut height

STEP 2

Cut the main and lining fabric. In this example, I would cut the main fabric 77″ × 23″. Use the main fabric size as a starting point to determine the size of the lining: subtract 4″ from the cut width and 6″ from the cut height. For this example, I would cut the lining 73″ × 17″.

Main fabric cut width − 4″ = _____ lining cut width

Main fabric cut height − 6″ = _____ lining cut height

Construction

STEP 1

Fold and press a 3″ double-fold hem along the bottom edge of your valance fabric. Unfold. Fold and press a 1″ double-fold hem along both short side edges. Unfold. **FIGURE A**

STEP 2

Make a mitered corner. To start, find the first point where the inner pressing lines intersect. **FIGURE B**

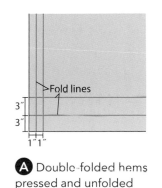

A Double-folded hems pressed and unfolded

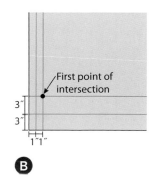

B

Fold up the bottom corner at that point, so the pressing lines line up with one another at a 45° angle. **FIGURE C**

Fold the side edge inward on the pressed line. Fold again, checking to make sure that the original point is now the mitered corner. **FIGURE D**

Fold up the hem once, then again, completing the mitered corner. **FIGURE E**

STEP 3

Use a whipstitch to hold the mitered corner in place, being careful not to sew through the front of the fabric. Continue to miter the remaining bottom corner. **FIGURES F & G**

STEP 4

On the back of the valance, slide the lining into the folded edges of the side and bottom hems on the main fabric. Pin in place. Using a whipstitch, hand stitch the lining to the main fabric, being careful not to sew through the front of the valance.

STEP 5

To add pleats, start by using an erasable fabric marking pen to mark the center of the valance. Next, measure and mark 7½″ from each finished end. **FIGURE H**

Measure and mark 4″ to each side of each of these 3 markings. **FIGURE I**

Working on the right side of valance, fold each of these 4″ markings in toward the original markings so that both meet

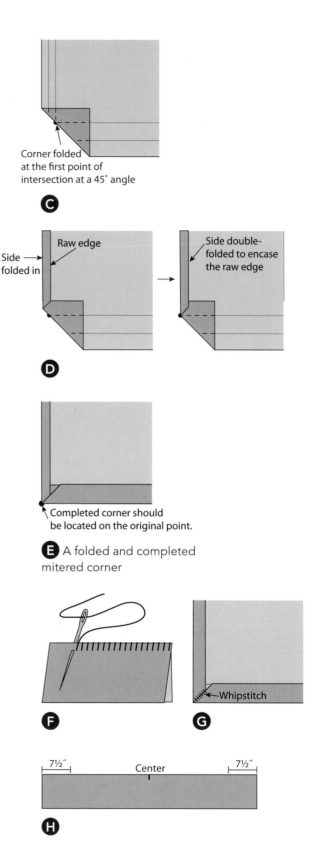

Corner folded at the first point of intersection at a 45° angle

C

Side folded in → Raw edge

Side double-folded to encase the raw edge

D

Completed corner should be located on the original point.

E A folded and completed mitered corner

F

←Whipstitch

G

7½″   Center   7½″

H

at the first mark. From the back, stitch a straight line from the top edge down 3″ on each outer pleat line to hold the pleated shape when the valance is attached to the board. **FIGURE J**

Congratulations! You have pleats! Baste these pleats along the top edge to hold them in position and press well. **FIGURE K**

STEP 6

Use some extra lining fabric to wrap the cut board as you would a present, stapling the lining in place as you go. **FIGURE L**

Lining wrap = 11″ × (board cut length + 6″)

Tip • I prefer to add the staples on the top of the board, so they won't be seen from below when the valance is installed.

STEP 7

Mark a line 2″ from the top of the valance. Align the mark with the top edge of the wrapped wood piece. Starting in the center, wrap the 2″ over the top of the board and staple in place. The pleats on either end should line up with the corners of the board, and the edges should extend to the back of the board. Staple well. **FIGURE M**

STEP 8

To install the valance, add 3–5 L-brackets on the bottom side of the board. Mark the L-bracket screw openings on the wall while a helper holds the valance level. Use appropriate screws and wall anchors for the wall type to ensure a secure install.

4″ 4″   4″ 4″   4″ 4″

I

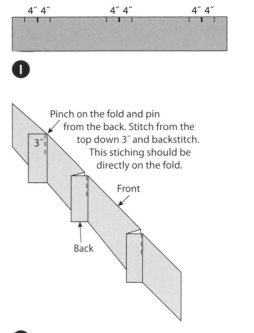

Pinch on the fold and pin from the back. Stitch from the top down 3″ and backstitch. This stiching should be directly on the fold.

3″

Front

Back

J Folds are shown with slight spacing for clarity. They should butt up against each other when placed correctly and stitched.

Basting stitch

K After stitching, flatten each pleat and press well.

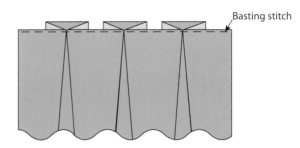

Staples

L

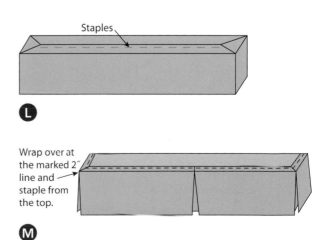

Wrap over at the marked 2″ line and staple from the top.

M

Cornice Board

FINISHED SIZE: Custom

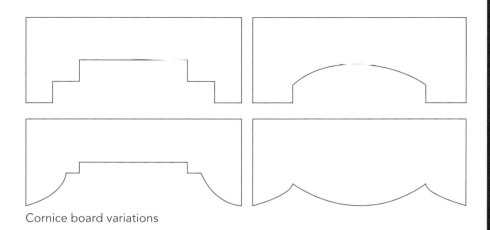

Cornice board variations

Materials and Supplies

- Any home decor fabric or quilting-weight cotton will work for this project (Determine the yardage requirements based on the size of the cornice board.)

- High-loft polyester batting

- ½″ plywood board at least as big as the desired cornice (See Measuring and Cutting, Step 2, below, to determine the size.)

- 1″ × 4″ wooden board, 2 times the height of your desired cornice (Use a 1″ × 6″ board if you'd like to mount panels under the cornice board.)

- 6–8 L-brackets, 3″ wide

- Wood glue

- Screws and screwdriver

- Staple gun and extra staples

- Jigsaw

Measuring and Cutting

STEP 1

Choose the style/shape of cornice board you'd like to use. It can be an example from the book or another shape you like.

STEP 2

Measure the window. Add 4″ to the width. The height of most cornice boards is typically around ⅛ to ⅙ of the height of the window.

Believe it or not, making a shaped cornice board requires no sewing. For a starter project, try a simple rectangle, then branch out from there. The possibilities for shapes are endless. Here are a few ideas to get you started.

Techniques Learned/Practiced

- **Using basic upholstery techniques**

STEP 3

Draw the outline of these dimensions on the ½" plywood, so that you know the size. Then draw the cornice board shape within this outline.

STEP 4

Using a jigsaw and safe cutting techniques, cut out the desired shape from the plywood.

STEP 5

From the 1" × 4" board, cut 2 lengths the same height as the ends of the cornice board. Attach the boards to either edge of the plywood cornice board shape. Use the L-brackets and wood glue to hold them in place.

Construction

STEP 1

Using a thick polyester batting, wrap the board and sides and staple the batting in place on the back. Cut out a piece of fabric larger than the cut board. Make sure you cut enough to wrap around the sides and over to the back as well.

Working on a clean surface, place the fabric right side down, then place the cornice board on top. Starting in the middle, pull the fabric taut around the top and bottom edges of the board and staple it in place. Repeat, moving from the middle of the cornice out toward one side and then the other, stapling the fabric at the top and bottom as you go. Continue alternating sides and working your way around the cornice board edge until all edges are wrapped and secured.

Alternating sides
stapled

Wrapped batting

Fabric, right side out

STEP 2

Trim off any extra fabric. Attach 2 L-brackets to each side of the cornice. Grab a helper and a level, and hang the cornice so the top is just a few inches above the window.

Tips

• *Add nailhead trim or tassels for a dressed-up cornice board.*

• *Be sure to use the right type of screw or other fasteners for the type of wall where you are attaching the cornice—you may need molly bolts or another type of wall anchor if you are not able to attach the brackets to a wooden stud.*

Drapes

FINISHED SIZE: Custom

Full-length drapes require a bit more fabric but look beautiful when completed. Start by making a simple lined drape, then learn how to add grommets or make elegant goblet pleats. Follow Steps 1–4, and then choose if you'd like to leave it as a simple drape and hang it with clip-on rings, or if you'd like to add grommets or goblet pleats to dress up the drape.

Techniques Learned/Practiced

- Lining a drape
- Adding grommets
- Using goblet pleat tape

Materials and Supplies

- Any weight home decor fabric and appropriate lining (Refer to Measuring and Cutting, Step 1, below, to determine the yardage by the size of the window and length of the drape.)

- Lining fabric

- Drapery rod, finials, and mounting brackets

- Grommet tape, same-sized grommets, and setting tool (optional)

- Goblet pleat tape, drapery hooks, and rings (optional)

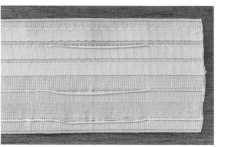
Goblet pleat tape

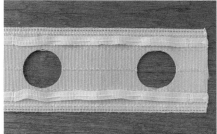
Grommet tape

Measuring and Cutting

STEP 1

Determine the finished length of the drapery panel. Also determine the finished width of the fabric you wish to use.

Note: Many people choose the width of the drapery panel based on the width of the home decor fabric they have chosen, most typically 50″–60″ wide. If you use one width of fabric per panel and add pleats or grommets, you would have a panel approximately 25″ wide. This is a good width for a stationary panel that's decorative only and won't ever be pulled closed. If you want a fully functioning drape, make the total width of the panels 2–2½ times the width of the window before you add pleats or grommets.

STEP 2

To determine the cut length of the main fabric, add 15½″ to the finished drape length. Trim off the selvages. You can use this width for 1 panel, or add another length of fabric to make a wider panel.

Finished drape length + 15½″ = _____ main fabric cut length

To determine the cut length of the lining fabric, add 1″ to the finished drape length. For the cut width of the lining, subtract 4″ from the main fabric width.

Finished drape length + 1″ = _____ lining cut length

Finished drape width − 4″= _____ lining cut width

Grommet-top drapes

Construction

Use a ½″ seam for all sewing.

STEP 1

Referring to Double-Fold Hem (page 23), make a 3″ double-fold hem along the bottom of each main fabric panel. Press well. Finish with a blind hem (page 24). Press well. Set aside.

Make a 1″ double-fold hem along the bottom of the lining fabric. Press well. Finish with a blind hem.

STEP 2

Place the main fabric, right side up, on a large flat surface with the hem nearest you. Place the hemmed lining, right side down, on top of the main fabric. Align the long edges along the right side and arrange the lining so the hem falls 1″ above the bottom of the main fabric hem. Stitch along the right edge. **FIGURE A**

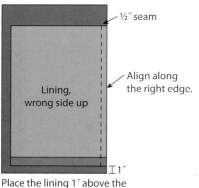

½″ seam

Align along the right edge.

Lining, wrong side up

1″

Place the lining 1″ above the main fabric bottom hem.

A

STEP 3

Pull the left edge of the lining over to align with the left side of the main fabric. Double check to make sure the hemmed edge of the lining falls 1″ above the main fabric hem. Stitch the left side. Turn right side out and press both sides well. The main fabric will wrap around to the back 1″ on either side. *Note that the top of the lining fabric will be below the top of the main fabric!* **FIGURE B**

Lining

Main fabric wrapped around to back

B

STEP 4

On the back of the drape, note where the raw edge of the main fabric is exposed and showing under the lining hem. Fold the bottom point of the raw edge diagonally up and under the main fabric side fold to conceal it. Hand stitch the diagonal fold to the main fabric hem to simulate a mitered corner. **FIGURE C**

STEP 5

To finish the header, press the top of the main fabric down 4¾″, then fold down again, enclosing the raw edges of the main fabric and lining. Press well.

- If you want your drapes to have a relaxed look, you can edgestitch (page 22) the top fold in place, then attach clips and hang. You are done!

- If you want to add grommets or goblet pleats, don't edgestitch the top fold yet! Instead, continue on with the following instructions.

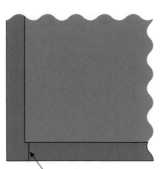

Raw edge of the main fabric showing beneath the lining hem

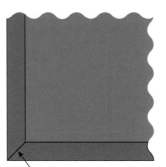

Fold up and under.

C Fold up the corner and stitch the underside seam in place.

STEP 6

Choose grommets (Step 7a) or goblet pleats (Steps 7b–10) for your header.

Grommet-top drapes

Pleated-top drapes

STEP 7A

To attach the grommets, align the top of the grommet tape ¼″ away from the folded top edge on the wrong side of the drape, with the center space between 2 grommet holes matching the center of the panel. Stitch the grommet tape on top of the header using the marked stitch lines as a guide. Fold one end under ½″ and stitch in place. Pull free the pull cords, then fold under the final end and stitch. Tie up one end of the pull cords. **FIGURE D**

Using the opening in the grommet tape as a guide, cut out the circles through all layers of the main fabric and lining. Install grommets into the openings using a setting tool and following the instructions on the package. Adjust the gathers with the pull cords if desired.

Hang on a rod to install.

End folded under ½″

Center the space between 2 grommet holes over the center of the panel top.

Tie ends

Keep pull threads clear of the end, then fold under the tape and stitch.

D

Note: If you are using a thicker fabric with lining, the plastic grommets that snap together may not work. You'll need metal grommets with a setting tool. Try folding a scrap of your fabric several times and setting a grommet to make sure the combination will work.

STEP 7B

To attach the goblet pleat tape, place the tape on top of the folded top edge on the wrong side of the drape. Center it on the panel top, using the stitched center marks as a guide. Stitch the tape in place on the top and bottom, following the indicated stitching lines. Stop about ½″ from each edge. **FIGURE E**

Stitch all edges.

Center the repeat mark on the panel center.

Pull out all 4 cords (3 thick and 1 thin cord) and the tie.

E

STEP 8

Fold one end under ½″ and stitch in place, taking care to backstitch well over all 4 cords—the 3 thick cords and 1 thin cord. Pull free the pull cords on the opposite side and tie together, then fold under this end and stitch.

STEP 9

Pull the 1 narrower cord first to gather the base sections of the goblet pleat, then pull the 3 thicker pull cords to form the pleats.

STEP 10

Slide a drapery hook into the top of each goblet pleat, as well as each side edge of the drape. Hook these into the drapery rings already on the rod.

Note: The instructions that come with the goblet pleat tape say to pull the 3 thick cords first, then the thin one. But I prefer to pull the thin cord first, then the 3 thick ones. It's easier!

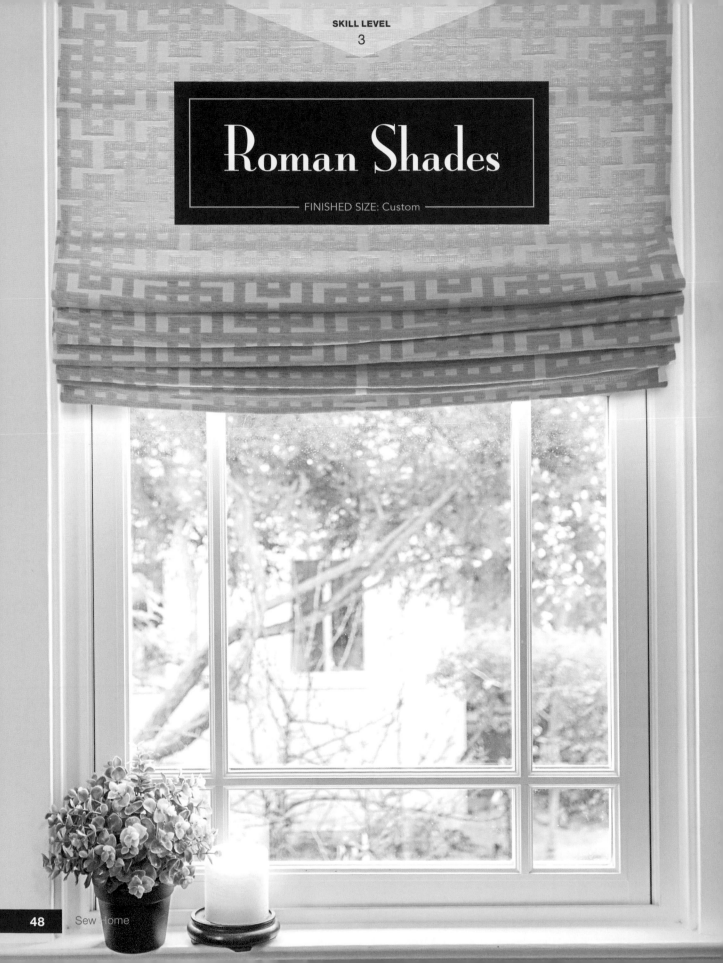

Roman Shades

FINISHED SIZE: Custom

Materials and Supplies

- Medium- or heavyweight home decor fabric

- Lining fabric, including extra to wrap the mounting board

- Roman shade tube tape

- Screw eyes

- Wall cleat

- Cord pull

- 12–15 yards of drapery cording, about 1/16″ thick by a length equal to 1½ × (height of shade + width of shade) × the number of vertical cords you're using

- L-brackets for mounting, 1 for each end plus 1 for every 14″ or so of window width

- ¾″ × 1½″ piece of wood, cut ¼″–⅜″ smaller than the window opening for the mounting board

- 5–8 dowel rods, 3/16″ diameter (If you need a width wider than the dowel rod, purchase and use Roman shade ribbing.)

- Invisible monofilament thread

- Coordinating polyester thread

- Fabric marking pen

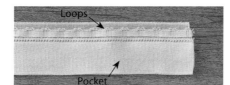
Roman shade tube tape

Measuring and Cutting

STEP 1

These roman shades will be mounted inside the window, so it's important to accurately measure the window. Don't round to the nearest ½″; use ⅛″–¼″ instead. Measure the width in a few places, because the width could be slightly different from the bottom to the top, and use the smallest width for your calculations.

STEP 2

Cut the main fabric and the lining fabric:

Finished width + 1″ = _____ cut width

Finished length + 6″ = _____ cut length

To cover the mounting board, cut a piece of lining fabric:

Window width + 2″ = _____ cut width

6″ = cut length

Construction

All seams are ½˝ unless noted otherwise.

STEP 1

To attach the tube tape, place the lining flat in front of you, right side up. Measure up 6˝ from the bottom and mark a horizontal line. From the first line, measure up and mark lines 8˝ apart until you are 14˝–18˝ from the top of the shade lining. **FIGURE A**

Align the top/loop edge of the tube tape with each line. Stitch ⅛˝ from the top edge, taking care not to sew the loops down. **FIGURE B**

STEP 2

To hem the sides and bottom of the shade, place the main fabric and lining right sides together and pin along both sides and the bottom. Stitch together using a ½˝ seam. Trim the corners, turn right side out, and press well.

STEP 3

To complete the rod tubes, place the shade on a flat surface and smooth it out. Pin the tube tape to the shade. Starting at the bottom, stitch the tube tape to the shade through both layers. Use coordinating bobbin and top thread for this step, because the stitching will show on the shade front. Using a clear thread is ideal. Refer to Choosing Thread (page 20). **FIGURE C**

After stitching each row, smooth the fabric before sewing the next seam to make sure that your fabric and lining are still lying flat and smooth. Pin if needed.

STEP 4

On the lining, mark vertical lines 2˝ from each edge of the shade and another line down the center. Along each line, use a large tapestry needle to run a line of cording through the loops in the tube tape. Each cord should be long enough to run from the bottom to the top of the shade, over to the left side (the right side when the shade is mounted) and back down to the bottom. Allow an extra foot or two for knots and adjustments. **FIGURE D**

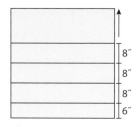

A Stop the 8˝ marks when you are 14˝–18˝ from the top of the lining.

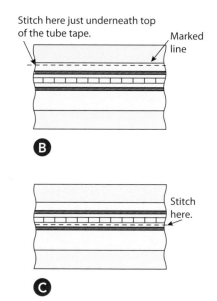

Stitch here just underneath top of the tube tape.

Marked line

B

Stitch here.

C

Tie the cording to the tube-tape loop at the bottom to secure.

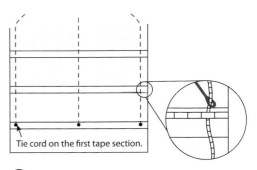

Tie cord on the first tape section.

D

STEP 5

Cut the dowel rods ¼″–⅜″ less than the finished shade width and slide them into the tube tape sleeves through the openings at the bottom of the tape. **FIGURE E**

STEP 6

Cut the mounting board about ¼″–½″ smaller than the finished shade width. Use the remaining lining fabric to cover and wrap the board just as you would a present, and staple where needed along a 1½″ flat side.

STEP 7

Use the same distances for running the cording in Step 4 to attach screw eyes into the side of the mounting board opposite from where you placed the staples. Sometimes it helps to lightly hammer the eyes to get them started, then begin to screw. **FIGURE F**

Tip • For a larger window, you will need more than 3 columns of cording to support the weight of the shade. I usually put the first 2 lines 2″ away from each side edge. Then I determine how many I will need in the center, making sure they are no more than 15″ or 16″ apart. I center those cords across the width of the shade.

STEP 8

Lay out the shade flat on your work surface, right side down. Measuring up from the finished hem, mark the finished length (the window height) along the top of the shade. Line up this marked line with the top edge of the mounting board and staple it in place along the top edge. Trim off any extra fabric.

Tip • You may want to put just a few staples on each end and the middle, then hold the shade up to the window to double-check the length and to make sure it's hanging level before you finish stapling it to the board.

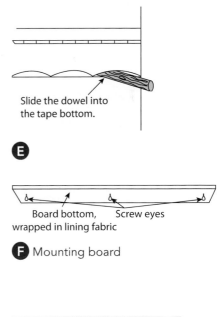

Slide the dowel into the tape bottom.

E

Board bottom, wrapped in lining fabric   Screw eyes

F Mounting board

STEP 9

On the lining side of the shade, continue threading the cording up through each screw eye and off to the left, which will be on the right when you view the shade from the front. Tie a loose knot in the cording to hold it together. Use the L-brackets to hang the shades, then adjust the cords so that the shade is hanging evenly. Thread through the cord pulls. Adjust so that the cords are even and then knot the cording. Mount the wall cleat.

Note: I usually mount my wall cleat inside the window.

4

Linens

With some quick tips and favorite cottons you can spruce up a wide variety of linens for bedrooms, bathrooms, and kitchens. No need to start from scratch for some of these! Use the following projects to add stylish customization to towels, sheets, and more. Along with sprucing up your home, you'll learn important techniques like making twisted pleats, designing knife-edge pillows, adding metal grommets, and sewing buttonholes.

54

57

73

75

60

64

68

70

77

80

83

85

4: Linens

53

BEDROOMS

Customized Sheets

FINISHED SIZE: Custom

Material and Supplies

- Nondirectional cotton fabric (See the table below for yardage requirements.)

- Purchased cotton sheet set

Customized Sheets

Flat Sheet Size	Yardage*
Twin and XL Twin	2¼ yards
Full	2⅝ yards
Queen	2⅞ yards
King and Cal King	3⅓ yards

*This table is based on standard sizing. Check the exact width of the top edge of the flat sheet and add 6″–12″ to calculate the yardage necessary for the sheet width to allow for shrinkage. You will have some extra fabric; save it to make coordinating pillowcases or shams!

Note: Before getting started, prewash both the accent fabric and sheet set and press well. Prewashing the fabrics will let them shrink and stabilize. If you skip this step, the accent fabric may shrink differently from the sheet set the first time you wash it, and you will end up with a puckered sheet.

Measuring and Cutting

STEP 1

Measure the exact width of the flat sheet. Add 1″ to the width.

STEP 2

From the accent fabric, cut a strip along the length of the fabric 19″ × the width you calculated in Step 1. Remember to remove the selvage before measuring and cutting.

Making custom sheets is always tricky. No one wants to feel a seam in the middle of the bed, and it's hard to find fabric wide enough to make sheets for anything larger than a crib. Don't let this keep you from having customized sheets! I'll show you how with only three seams. Purchase any size of a coordinating sheet set and follow the instructions to add a favorite fabric to coordinate with the bedroom.

Techniques Learned/Practiced

- Cutting large pieces of fabric

Construction

All seams are ½˝ unless noted otherwise.

STEP 1

Along each short edge of the accent fabric, fold ½˝ to the wrong side and press well.

STEP 2

Trim off the top folded fabric seam from the purchased flat sheet. **FIGURE A**

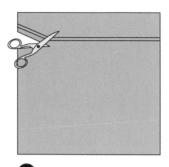

A Trim the top finished edge from the sheet.

STEP 3

Place the accent fabric strip on a flat surface, right side up. The ½˝ folded and pressed edges should still be folded. Line up the cut edge of the sheet top with the top edge of the accent fabric. Pin generously. Roll up the sheet until approximately half of the accent fabric strip is exposed. Fold up the other long edge of the accent fabric strip to meet the already pinned raw edge, right sides together. Pin in place. Now you've created a tube of accent fabric around the rolled-up sheet. Stitch along the pinned edge. **FIGURE B**

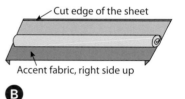

Cut edge of the sheet

Accent fabric, right side up

B

> **Design Note:** If you choose to use a fabric with a directional print, place the accent strip with the fabric pattern pointing up when beginning Step 3. This placement will ensure that the fabric will lie in the right direction when the sheet is tucked in and folded down.

STEP 4

Pull out the rolled sheet and continue turning the tube until the accent fabric is also right side out. Press along the previously sewn seam. Refold and press the ½˝ sides as needed. Edgestitch (page 22) both edges to close up the sides. Press the top once more. There you have it! Three seams and you've customized some coordinated sheets, easy-peasy.

Fancy Flange Shams

FINISHED SIZE: Boudoir: 21″ × 17″ • Standard: 31″ × 25″ • King: 41″ × 25″ • Euro: 31″ × 31″

Making a flange sham is actually quite simple—so simple that you'll be left wondering why you haven't made a bunch! These can be made with appropriate home decor fabric or a favorite cotton print. If the fabric you choose is lightweight or medium-lightweight, use a woven fusible interfacing or thin cotton batting as interfacing. This will keep the flanges from flopping about.

Techniques Learned/Practiced

- Making an envelope pillow closure
- Sewing a flange

Materials, Supplies, and Cutting

Use the table below to determine the size, yardage requirements, and starting pieces for some standard sham sizes.

- Any type of fabric (If you choose a fairly lightweight fabric, use a lightweight woven interfacing on the back to give it more body.)
- Fabric marking pen
- Pillow form

Fancy Flange Shams

Sham Type	Pillow Form	Yardage (based on 42″ width/54″ width)	Cut Pieces (Pieces are listed width × height so you can cut directional prints correctly.)
Boudoir	16″ × 12″	1⅛ yards / 1 yard	Cut 1 rectangle 22″ × 18″ for front. Cut 2 rectangles 15″ × 18″ for back.
Standard	26″ × 20″	1⅝ yards / 1⅝ yards	Cut 1 rectangle 32″ × 26″ for front. Cut 2 rectangles 20″ × 26″ for back.
King	36″ × 20″	2⅝ yards / 2¼ yards	Cut 1 rectangle 42″ × 26″ for front. Cut 2 rectangles 24″ × 26″ for back.
Euro	26″ × 26″	2⅛ yards / 2 yards	Cut 1 square 32″ × 32″ for front. Cut 2 rectangles 20″ × 32″ for back.

Tip • Typically, you'd use 1 sham for a twin or full bed, 2 for a queen, and 3 for a king.

Construction

Follow these instructions for any size. All seams are ½″ unless noted otherwise.

STEP 1

On each back rectangle, make a ½″ double-fold hem (page 23) on one long side. Finish the hem with an edge stitch (page 22). Set aside.

STEP 2

Place the front piece right side up on a flat surface. Place both back pieces right sides down on top of this piece, with the hemmed edges overlapping in the center of the pillow. Match up all outside, top, and bottom raw edges. Pin well. **FIGURE A**

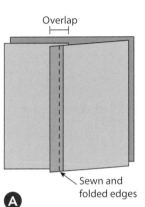

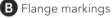

A Sewn and folded edges

STEP 3

Stitch around the perimeter of the pillow. Trim excess fabric from the corners. Turn right side out through the opening where the back pieces overlap. Press well. Use a fabric marking pen and a straight-edge ruler to mark lines 2½″ inside each outer edge. **FIGURE B**

Tip • If a fabric marking pen is too hard to see, use a row of removable tape (like washi tape or painter's tape) to mark the stitching line.

Stitch directly on this line (or next to the tape) around the entire exterior of the pillow.

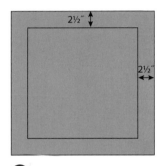

B Flange markings

STEP 4

Add the pillow form through the back opening and place the pillow on the bed. You're finished!

Tip • Design Option: Add a decorative ribbon or twill tape to the sewn flange line.

Bed Skirt

FINISHED SIZES, EACH WITH A 14″ DROP:

- Twin: 189″ × 14″ for a mattress 39″ × 75″
- XL Twin: 199″ × 14″ for a mattress 39″ × 80″
- Full: 204″ × 14″ for a mattress 54″ × 75″
- Queen: 220″ × 14″ for a mattress 60″ × 80″
- King: 236″ × 14″ for a mattress 76″ × 80″
- Cal King: 240″ × 14″ for a mattress 72″ × 84″

Materials, Supplies, and Cutting

Refer to the table below for the fabric and trim yardages required for the bed skirt size you choose to make.

- Any midweight to heavyweight cotton or upholstery fabric

- 1–2 packages of upholstery twist pins

- Decorative trim (See the table below for yardage requirements.)

Bed Skirt

Bed Size	Fabric	Trim	Cut Pieces (Pieces are listed width × height so you can cut directional prints correctly.)
Twin	3½ yards main fabric	6 yards	Cut 2 rectangles 77″ × 18″ for sides. Cut 1 rectangle 41″ × 18″ for end. Cut 2 rectangles 8″ × 18″ for split corners.
XL Twin	3½ yards main fabric	6¼ yards	Cut 2 rectangles 82″ × 18″ for sides. Cut 1 rectangle 41″ × 18″ for end. Cut 2 rectangles 8″ × 18″ for split corners.
Full	3⅞ yards main fabric	6½ yards	Cut 2 rectangles 77″ × 18″ for sides. Cut 1 rectangle 56″ × 18″ for end. Cut 2 rectangles 8″ × 18″ for split corners.
Queen	4¼ yards main fabric	7 yards	Cut 2 rectangles 82″ × 18″ for sides. Cut 1 rectangle 62″ × 18″ for end. Cut 2 rectangles 8″ × 18″ for split corners.

Table continued on page 62.

Learn how to make a bed skirt quickly and easily, as well as how to secure it in place so it's not constantly askew. The instructions allow for a 14″ drop, which is typical. Measure the distance from the top of your box spring to the floor, and adjust if necessary. Also measure your mattress and adjust the width of each section of the bed skirt if needed.

Techniques Learned/Practiced

- Attaching a bed skirt that doesn't slip or shift

- Attaching decorative trim

Bed Size	Fabric	Trim	Cut Pieces (Pieces are listed width × height so you can cut directional prints correctly.)
King	4¾ yards main fabric	7½ yards	Cut 2 rectangles 82″ × 18″ for sides. Cut 1 rectangle 78″ × 18″ for end. Cut 2 rectangles 8″ × 18″ for split corners.
Cal King	4⅝ yards main fabric	7⅜ yards	Cut 2 rectangles 86″ × 18″ for sides. Cut 1 rectangle 74″ × 18″ for end. Cut 2 rectangles 8″ × 18″ for split corners.

Tip • *Try finding a flat sheet or premade drapery curtains to cut the pieces from. Many times this will be less expensive than buying fabric yardage, especially for the larger bed skirts.*

Construction

Follow these instructions for any size. All seams are ½″ unless noted otherwise.

STEP 1

For each cut piece, measure up and mark a line 3½″ from the bottom edge. Align the bottom edge of the trim with the marked line. Using a clear monofilament thread, stitch the trim to each piece.

Note: On the side and end pieces, the bottom edge will be a long side. On the split corner pieces, the bottom edge will be a short side. The 18″ sides are for the height of the bed skirt.

STEP 2

Make a ½″ double-fold hem (page 23) around all 4 edges of each side, end, and split corner rectangle. Fold in, press, and edgestitch (page 22) the side edges first, then the top and bottom edges.

Mark the center of each corner piece. Arrange all pieces as shown. Place the side and bottom pieces on top of the corner pieces, meeting at the center mark. Stitch a ½″ line along the top of the split corner sections to secure them to the side and bottom pieces.

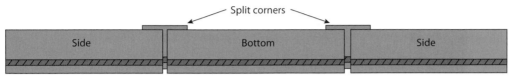

It will be one *long* piece when completed.

STEP 3

Remove the mattress from the bed. Use the upholstery twist pins to secure both corners to the box spring frame. Then work your way around each side. To apply the twist pins, use a small hammer or rubber mallet to get the point started slightly, then twist the pin down into the box spring frame.

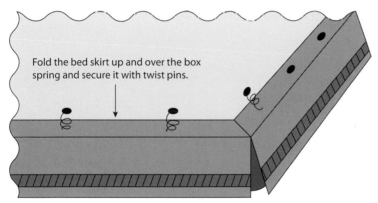

Fold the bed skirt up and over the box spring and secure it with twist pins.

The top of the bed skirt seam should fold up and over the edge of the box spring approximately 2″.

You're finished!

Tip: Design Options

• *Make your own trim by cutting 4″ accent fabric strips. Fold down both long edges ½″ and press well. Pin and stitch in place as you would the trim.*

• *Forgo the accent trim/fabric altogether and use an accent fabric for the 2 split corner sections instead.*

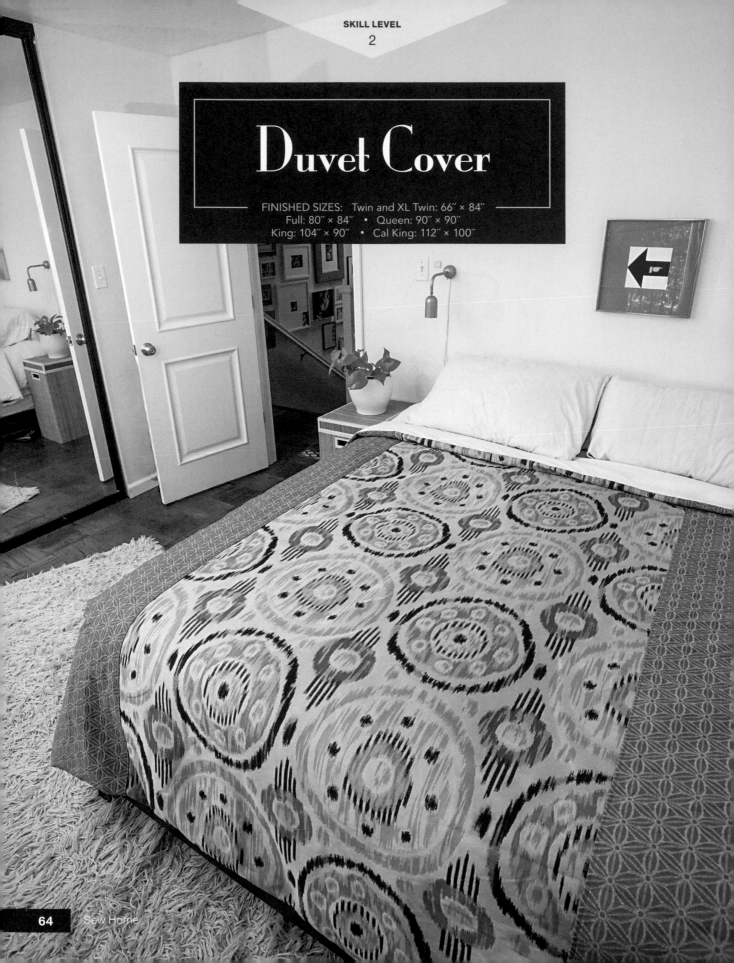

Duvet Cover

FINISHED SIZES: Twin and XL Twin: 66″ × 84″
Full: 80″ × 84″   •   Queen: 90″ × 90″
King: 104″ × 90″   •   Cal King: 112″ × 100″

Notes

- Measure your comforter before starting, and adjust the finished size of the cover if necessary.

- For queen- and king-sized duvet covers, you may need to piece lengths of fabric to create the width you need.

- Consider using extra-wide fabric meant for quilt backing, which comes in 90″–108″ widths; use the extra width for pillows or a bed skirt!

Materials, Supplies, and Cutting

- Main, accent, and backing fabrics (See the table below for yardage requirements.)

- 2 yards of twill tape, ½″ wide

- 8–14 coordinating buttons, 1″

Duvet Cover

Bed Size	Yardage (42″ width)	Cut Pieces
Twin & XL Twin	2½ yards main fabric	Cut 1 rectangle 29″ × 85″.
	2½ yards accent fabric	Cut 2 rectangles 20″ × 85″.
	5¼ yards backing fabric	Cut 2 rectangles 34″ × 93″.
Full	2½ yards main fabric	Cut 1 rectangle 37″ × 85″.
	5 yards accent fabric (2½ yards if fabric is wider than 48″)	Cut 2 rectangles 23″ × 85″.
	5¼ yards backing fabric	Cut 2 rectangles 41″ × 93″.
Queen	2¾ yards main fabric	Cut 1 rectangle 43″ × 91″.
	5¼ yards accent fabric (2¾ yards if fabric is wider than 52″)	Cut 2 rectangles 25″ × 91″.
	5¾ yards backing fabric (48″+ wide)	Cut 2 rectangles 46″ × 99″.

Table continued on page 66.

If you have a hard time finding a coordinating duvet cover for your favorite bedroom, this project is for you! You'll be dealing with some large pieces of fabric, but the sewing is very straightforward.

Techniques Learned/Practiced

- Making buttonholes
- Stitching on buttons

Bed Size	Yardage (42″ width)	Cut Pieces
King	2¾ yards main fabric (53″+ wide)	Cut 1 rectangle 51″ × 91″.
	2¾ yards accent fabric (60″+ wide) OR 5¼ yards accent fabric (less than 60″ wide)	Cut 2 rectangles 28″ × 91″.
	5¾ yards backing fabric (55″+ wide)	Cut 2 rectangles 53″ × 99″.
Cal King	3 yards main fabric (53″+ wide)	Cut 1 rectangle 51″ × 101″.
	3 yards accent fabric (66″+ wide) OR 5¾ yards accent fabric (less than 66″ wide)	Cut 2 rectangles 32″ × 101″.
	6¼ yards backing fabric (60″ wide)	Cut 2 rectangles 57″ × 109″.

Construction

Follow these instructions for any size. All seams are ½″ unless noted otherwise.

STEP 1

Stitch an accent fabric rectangle to either long side of the main fabric rectangle. Press seams flat to one side. Set aside.

Note: I usually press the seams toward the accent fabric, but if your accent fabric is light, you could press seams toward the main fabric. If the seam does not stay flat after pressing, you could topstitch ¼″ from the seam to hold it in place.

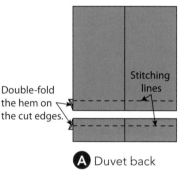

Double-fold the hem on the cut edges.

Stitching lines

A Duvet back

STEP 2

Align both backing rectangles along a long edge and stitch together to make a large backing piece. Cut a 10″ strip from the bottom of the backing piece.

Make a 1½″ double-fold hem on the edges you just cut on both the backing piece and the 10″ backing strip. Edgestitch (page 22) the hems in place. **FIGURE A**

STEP 3

On the backing piece, draw a line 1″ inside the edge of the stitched hem. Measure 4″ from either side of the center seam and mark on the line. Continue to mark on the line every 8″ from these first marks until you are within a few inches of the edge of the duvet. **FIGURE B**

Repeat with the hemmed edge of the 10″ backing strip.

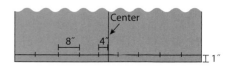

B Button and buttonhole alignment marks

STEP 4

Stitch buttons at each mark on the hemmed 10″ backing strip. Use a sewing machine with a buttonhole stitch and an automatic buttonhole foot to stitch buttonholes centered on each mark on the large backing piece. **FIGURE C**

Tip • You may want to practice stitching a few buttonholes on a scrap of fabric to see how your machine stitches buttonholes. Typically, the machine will start sewing at the bottom of the buttonhole, so it may be wise for you to start about ½″ from the center mark to make sure the buttonhole is in the appropriate place. When using an automatic buttonhole foot, place the button inside the foot and let the foot and machine do the rest!

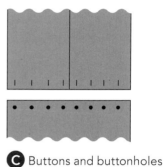

C Buttons and buttonholes

STEP 5

To finish the duvet, cut the 2 yards of twill tape into 4 equal pieces. Place the duvet front on a large surface, faceup. Fold each piece of twill tape in half and stitch to each of the 4 corners with a ⅜″ seam. The twill tape tails should face out, off the fabric. **FIGURE D**

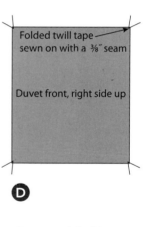

D

STEP 6

Place the duvet front, faceup, on a flat surface. Button the 2 backing sections together and place them facedown on top of the duvet front, aligning all 4 edges. Pin well. **FIGURE E**

Stitch around the entire duvet cover. Reach through and unbutton the back.

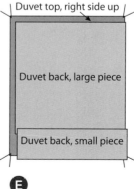

E

STEP 7

Place the comforter on top of the duvet; bunch up about 1½″ of each comforter corner and use the 4 pieces of twill tape to tie each comforter corner in place. Turn the cover right side out with the comforter tied in place inside. Button up the backing and it's ready for company!

BATHROOMS

Customized Bath and Hand Towels

FINISHED SIZE: Custom

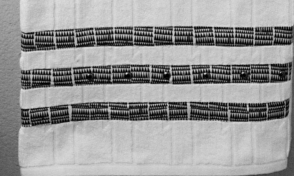

Materials and Supplies

- ⅜ yard of medium-weight cotton fabric for an accent, pre-washed
- Coordinating towel and hand towel, prewashed
- 15–20 metal dome hot-fix studs, 6mm
- 12–15 metal dome hot-fix studs, 10mm

Measuring and Cutting

STEP 1

Press the prewashed fabric well. Measure the width of the towel. Record this measurement and add 1″.

STEP 2

From the accent fabric, cut 3 strips 2″ × (towel width + 1″).

Construction

STEP 1

Press each long edge of the fabric strips ½″ to the wrong side to make strips 1″ wide.

Press each short edge ½″ to the wrong side.

STEP 2

Mark a parallel line 3″ from the bottom edge of the towel. From the first parallel line, mark 2 more parallel lines 2″ apart.

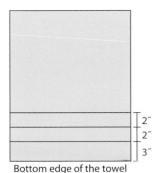

Bottom edge of the towel
Alignment markings on the towel

STEP 3

Align the folded bottom edge of each accent strip with a marked line, also aligning the short folded edges with the edges of the towel. Pin well. Using a coordinating thread color, edgestitch (page 22) around all 4 edges of the accent strips.

STEP 4

Make evenly spaced 2″ markings on the center strip. Place the 10mm hot-fix metal studs on the marks, centered within the height of the strip. To affix the studs to the fabric, you can use a tool made especially for hot-fix crystals and studs, or use a large clamshell press or an iron. Always use a pressing cloth

when using a press or an iron on these embellishments.

STEP 5

Repeat the same process with the hand towel, but with the following changes:

- Cut 3 accent strips 1″ × (towel width + 1″). Press each long edge under ¼″.

- Mark 1 parallel line 1¾″ from the bottom edge of the hand towel. From that line, mark 2 parallel lines 1¼″ apart.

- Stitch the accent strips in place and iron on the 6mm metal studs following the same instructions as the towel, but space the studs 1″ apart.

Shower Curtain

FINISHED SIZE: 72″ × 72″

Materials and Supplies

- 5¼ yards of fabric (more if matching a large-scale pattern)

- 12 grommets, 7/16″ and grommet setting tool

- Walking foot for sewing machine

Cutting

Cut the fabric in half horizontally, making 2 sections 2⅝ yards each. Trim off all selvages.

Construction

All seams are ½″ unless noted otherwise.

STEP 1

Match up 2 of the 2⅝-yard sides right sides together and pin well. Align the pattern of the fabric if needed by offsetting 1 side of the panel. Stitch together with a walking foot if you have one.

Offset if needed to match the pattern.

Techniques Learned/Practiced

- Installing metal grommets

STEP 2

From the seamed fabric from Step 1, cut a large rectangle 76″ × 88″. Refer to How to Cut Large Pieces of Fabric in a Limited Space (page 19).

STEP 3

On each 88″ side, fold and edgestitch (page 22) a 1″ double-fold hem (page 23).

At the top, fold and edgestitch a 4″ double-fold hem.

At the bottom, fold a 4″ double-fold hem and sew it with a blind hem stitch.

STEP 4

To mark the grommet placement, lay the top edge flat. Use an erasable fabric pen to draw a line 1½″ from the top, parallel to the top edge. Measure and mark 1″ from either side. Then measure and place additional marks every 6⅜″ across the width. Start from each end and work toward the center. Note that you will need to "use up" an extra ⅛″ across the width of the fabric; you can do this by moving the 2 marks at the ends a hair (¹⁄₁₆″) toward the outside edges.

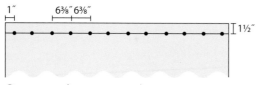

Grommet placement markings

STEP 5

Once you have the placement marked for the grommets, use the grommets to mark the cutting line. Center a grommet over each marking and trace the inside using a fabric marking pen. Use small pointed sharp scissors to trim through all layers.

STEP 6

Install the grommets by aligning all the pieces of the grommet and setting tool as shown. Hammer into place to secure.

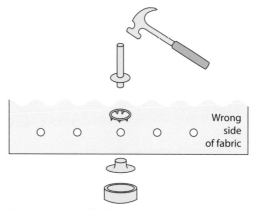

Grommet installation

Hang the curtain on the shower rod using shower hooks, and enjoy a nice steamy shower.

Floral Bath Mat

FINISHED SIZE: 20″ × 30″

Using floral fabric and a classy black-and-white stripe print, you will have this très chic new bath mat done in no time!

Techniques Learned/Practiced

- Basic appliquéing

Materials and Supplies

- 2–3 fat quarters or ½ yard of a floral fabric
- ⅔ yard of black-and-white striped fabric
- 1 standard bath towel in a coordinating color, at least 21″ × 31″, prewashed
- 1 yard of sewable fusible fabric adhesive

Cutting

STEP 1

Choose 7–10 of the flowers from the floral fabric. Cut a piece of fusible fabric adhesive slightly larger than each flower. Iron the fusible onto the wrong side of the fabric, then cut out the flower shape around its edges.

STEP 2

Cut a 21″ × 31″ rectangle from the black-and-white striped fabric. With right sides together, fold in half vertically and horizontally and press lightly. Unfold.

STEP 3

Trim the bath towel to 21″ × 31″.

Construction

STEP 1

Place the cut fabric flowers in an arrangement that's pleasing to you. I usually start with the larger ones in the center and work out toward the edges with the smaller-scale flowers. Use the pressed lines as a guide to keep everything centered. Iron in place when the arrangement is complete, following the manufacturer's instructions for the fusible adhesive.

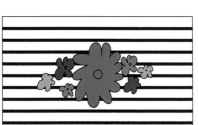

Floral arrangement

STEP 2

On the sewing machine, use a straight stitch or an appliqué stitch to secure the edges of the flowers.

Note: Start stitching on a straight section of the appliqué to make it easier to start and stop. Starting on a corner or curve can be more difficult.

STEP 3

Place the appliquéd piece and the trimmed towel right sides together, aligning all edges and corners. Pin well. Stitch around the perimeter, using a walking foot to keep the 2 layers from shifting. Leave a 4″–5″ opening along 1 side.

STEP 4

Turn right side out through the opening. Press the edges and topstitch around the mat ¼″ from the edge, enclosing the folded opening.

Add to your favorite bathroom and enjoy!

Quick and Easy Tablecloth

FINISHED SIZE: Custom

This is one of my favorite quick projects to change the look of my eating nook in the kitchen! With a few yards of fabric and less than an hour of your time, you can make a custom tablecloth. These instructions will work for any square or rectangular table.

Techniques Learned/Practiced

- Measuring and cutting accurately
- Finishing raw edges

Materials and Supplies

- Any light- to midweight washable home decor fabric, prewashed (Exact yardage will be determined based on the size of the table.)

Tip • Purchase extra fabric to allow for shrinkage.

Measuring and Cutting

STEP 1

Measure the table length and width. Add 12″ to each measurement to determine the cut size of your fabric. For example, if your table is 36″ × 42″, the cutting size will be 48″ × 54″. To calculate yardage, refer to Determining Yardage (page 17).

STEP 2

Piece the fabric if needed, then press and cut the piece according to the measurement determined in Step 1.

Construction

Use a serger or an overlock foot and corresponding stitch on the sewing machine to finish all 4 edges. Fold under ⅜″, press, and edgestitch (page 22).

That's it! Place your new tablecloth on the table and get it set for your next dinner party!

It's a Twist Table Runner

— FINISHED SIZE: 15″ × 48″ —

Use a favorite shot cotton, silk, or linen to make a simple yet elegant table runner. You'll learn how to make twisted wave pleats to add texture to the project.

Techniques Learned/Practiced

- **Making twisted pleats**

Materials and Supplies

- 1 yard of main fabric, 42″ wide
- ⅜ yard of contrasting fabric, 42″ wide
- ⅞ yard of backing fabric, 42″ wide
- 3 yards of lightweight woven fusible interfacing, 20″ wide
- Fabric marking pen

Cutting

From main fabric:

Cut 1 rectangle 30¾″ × 16″ for left side.

Cut 1 rectangle 8¾″ × 16″ for right side.

Cut 2 strips 2″ × 17″ for pleated section.

Cut 7 strips 1½″ × 17″ for pleated section.

From contrasting fabric:

Cut 8 strips 1½″ × 17″.

From backing:

Cut 2 rectangles 24½″ × 16″.

From interfacing:

Cut 1 rectangle 30¾″ × 16″ for left side.

Cut 1 rectangle 8¾″ × 16″ for right side.

Cut 1 rectangle 48½″ × 16″ for backing.

Cut 1 rectangle 10½″ × 16″ for pleated section.

Construction

All seams are ¼″ unless noted otherwise.

STEP 1

Piece together the backing rectangles along the 16″ edges to make a long rectangle. Iron a piece of woven fusible interfacing of the same size to the back. Set aside.

STEP 2

Fold all contrast pleat strips in half lengthwise, wrong sides together, and press well. Sandwich each folded section between the 1½″ and 2″ strips of main fabric as shown and stitch together to make a pleat base. The 2″ strips should be at the outsides.

Press all the seams to one side and trim the top and bottom edges so it is 16″ high. Iron the 16″ × 10½″ piece of fusible interfacing to the back to stabilize. **FIGURE A**

STEP 3

Fold, press, and pin all pleats to the left. Sew a basting stitch along the top and bottom edge to hold the pleats in one direction. **FIGURE B**

STEP 4

Mark stitching lines on the pleated piece. First, mark a line horizontally through the center of the table runner top. From the center line, mark 2 parallel lines above and 2 parallel lines below, each 3″ apart. Refer to the stitching diagram to note the stitching direction for each line. **FIGURE C**

Stitch the lines with a coordinating thread, taking care to push the pleats in the direction you are stitching. Because the direction alternates in each row, the pleats will fold differently, causing them to look twisted.

Tip • It will be easiest to sew the outer and center lines first, then switch and sew the other 2 lines in the opposite direction.

STEP 5

Iron the fusible interfacing rectangles to the back of the left and right main fabric rectangles.

Pin and stitch the left and right main fabric rectangles to the pleated center, right sides together. Press the seams well. **FIGURE D**

STEP 6

Place the top and bottom pieces right sides together and pin. Stitch around the outer edge using a ½″ seam, leaving a 5″ opening on one edge. Clip the corners, then turn right side out. Press the opening shut, then press all other edges flat. Edgestitch (page 22) all 4 edges.

You're finished!

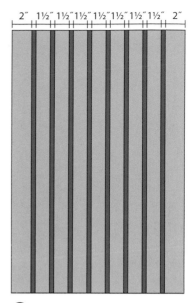

2″ 1½″ 1½″ 1½″ 1½″ 1½″ 1½″ 1½″ 2″

A Pleat base

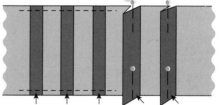

Pleats pressed and basted   Pleats pressed and pinned

B Pleats pressed, pinned, and basted to the left

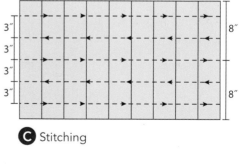

3″   8″
3″
3″
3″   8″

C Stitching

16″ × 30¾″   8¾″ × 16″

D Table runner assembly

Color–Blocked Place Mats

FINISHED SIZE: 12″ × 18″

Materials and Supplies

These supplies make a set of 4.

- 1 yard each of 3 coordinating fabrics A–C, 42″ wide

- 1 yard of backing fabric, 42″ wide

- 3 yards of lightweight woven interfacing (such as Pellon SF101), 20″ wide

- Fabric marking pen

Tip • Instead of using a solid fabric on the back, whip up a few more fronts and use them on the backs to make them reversible. I tend to group seasons/holidays together, so I can keep the same set of place mats out longer.

These place mats can be whipped up quickly in an endless variety of color combinations.

Techniques Learned/Practiced

- Simple piecing

- Practicing with color palettes

Cutting

From Fabric A:

Cut 2 rectangles 14″ × 16½″.

Cut 2 rectangles 12″ × 14″.

From Fabric B:

Cut 1 rectangle 14″ × 16½″.

Cut 3 rectangles 12″ × 14″.

From Fabric C:

Cut 1 rectangle 14″ × 16½″.

Cut 3 rectangles 12″ × 14″.

From backing:

Cut 4 rectangles 13″ × 19″.

From interfacing:

Cut 8 rectangles 13″ × 19″.

Additional Cutting:

On the bottom edge of each 14″ × 16½″ rectangle from fabrics A, B, and C, measure and mark 6½″ from the bottom left corner. Use a ruler and rotary cutter to trim an angle from this mark to the top right corner.

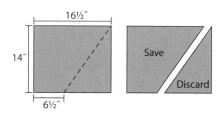

Construction

All seams are ¼″ unless noted otherwise.

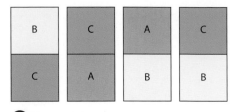

A Pairing guide

STEP 1

Piece together 2 small rectangles from fabrics B and C along the 12″ edges. Referring to the pairing guide (at right), piece together the remaining small rectangles. **FIGURE A**

Press the seams open (or to the darker side if you chose any fabrics in light colors).

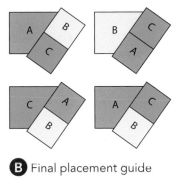

B Final placement guide

STEP 2

Pair up each pieced section from Step 1 with a large rectangle that's been cut at an angle. Align at the diagonal lines, right sides together, and pin. Before you sew, test to see that when stitched, the piece will allow for a 13″ × 19″ rectangle to be cut. You may have to slide the angled piece down a bit to better align with the angle on the rectangle. **FIGURE B**

Stitch and press. Trim each place mat front to 13″ × 19″. **FIGURE C**

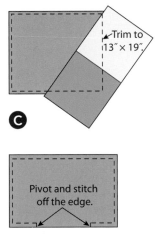

Trim to 13″ × 19″.

C

STEP 3

Iron the interfacing onto the back of the 4 pieced fronts and 4 backs.

Pin a front and a back right sides together. Stitch a ½″ seam around all 4 edges, leaving a 4″ opening along one edge. **FIGURE D**

Pivot and stitch off the edge.

D Pivot and stitch through the seam allowance at the opening to make it easier to edgestitch in the next step.

STEP 4

Clip the corners, turn right side out, press the opening closed, and edgestitch (page 22) around all outer edges, securing the opening. Press once more and you're finished.

Note: If you want a clean look on the edges, use a permanent fabric adhesive to close the opening instead of an edge stitch.

Tip • The place mats are best washed and air-dried. They will need to be pressed after washing. If you're worried about food stains, treat them with Scotchgard before use.

Rolled-Hem Napkins

FINISHED SIZE: 15½″ × 15½″

For this project you'll use a specialized rolled hem foot and your favorite quilting-weight cottons to make coordinated napkins that are both customized and earth-friendly.

Techniques Learned/Practiced

• Stitching a rolled hem

• Working with curves

Materials and Supplies

These supplies make 2 napkins.

• ½ yard quilting-weight cotton, prewashed

• Rolled hem foot for sewing machine

• Heavy starch spray

Cutting and Construction

STEP 1

After prewashing the fabric, cut 2 squares 16″ × 16″.

STEP 2

Fold each square in half horizontally and vertically. Use a large plate to round the corners of the napkin.

Unfold. Starch the edges well to make the hem easier to sew. This especially helps to keep the fabric from distorting on curved corners.

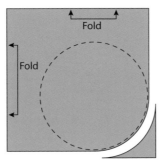

Fold the fabric and round the corner.

STEP 3

Starting on a straight edge, insert the edge of the fabric into the rolled portion of the presser foot. Unthread the needle and stitch forward with a straight stitch 1″–2″ while the fabric starts to fold and roll inward. Stop and thread the needle, then resume stitching to stitch the edge down. Carefully go around the curved corners until you end up close to where you began. When you are within 1″–2″ from the beginning, remove the fabric from the folded portion of the foot. The unstitched portion will want to go ahead and roll in. Roll it in and press. Stitch along the edge to complete the stitching.

Note: If you haven't sewn a rolled hem before, practice a few times on some scrap fabric. It won't take you long to be confident with the technique, and it's less stressful than starting right away on your project fabric.

Tip • Design Option: Use solid-color cotton and embellish the napkin edges with those infrequently used decorative stitches on the sewing machine.

Pineapple Hot Pad

— FINISHED SIZE: 9″ × 11″ —

Aloha! Make this tropical pineapple hot pad as a gift or for your own kitchen. You'll learn how to make the pineapple texture with a technique called prairie points.

Materials and Supplies

• ¼ yard or 1 fat quarter of green fabric

• ⅝ yard of yellow fabric

• 12″ × 12″ square of Insul-Fleece batting (C&T Publishing)

• 12″ × 12″ square of 100% cotton batting

• 12″ × 12″ square of backing fabric

Cutting

From yellow fabric:

Cut 2 rectangles 7″ × 10″.

Cut 75 squares 2½″ × 2½″.

From Insul-Fleece and batting:

Cut 1 rectangle 7″ × 10″ from each.

From green fabrics and cotton batting:

Trace the pineapple leaf pattern (next page) onto paper and cut it out to make a template. Use the template to cut 1 leaf and 1 reversed leaf from the green fabric and 1 layer of cotton batting.

Construction

All seams are ½″ unless noted otherwise.

STEP 1

Fold a yellow fabric square in half, wrong sides together. Then fold each corner down toward the raw edge to make a small triangle. Press well. Repeat with all remaining yellow squares. **FIGURE A**

STEP 2

Mark 2″ away from each corner of the 7″ × 10″ yellow fabric, backing fabric, and Insul-Fleece rectangles. Draw a diagonal line and cut off all corners. Discard the trimmed corner triangles. **FIGURE B**

STEP 3

Mark a horizontal line parallel to a short end of the yellow rectangle, ⅝″ from the top edge. Line up the folded yellow triangles at the top of the rectangle, making sure that the points don't go over the marked line and that they overlap slightly. Stitch along the bottom of the triangles to secure. Then add and stitch an overlapping row, placing the row about ⅝″ below the previous row. **FIGURE C**

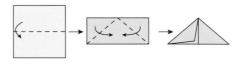

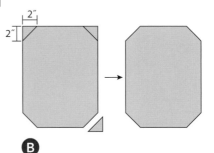

Ⓐ Making prairie points

Ⓑ

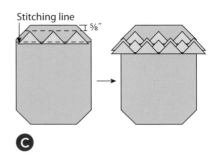

Stitching line ⅝″

Ⓒ

Continue layering the points as needed. It's okay if they hang off the side edges; just trim the sides when you're finished adding triangles. Once you've reached the bottom, set the unit aside.

STEP 4

Sandwich the green leaves and cotton batting together, with the right sides of the green fabric facing out and the cotton batting in the middle. Pin. Topstitch ⅛″ from the edge to secure all layers, giving the leaves a raw-edge finish. **FIGURE D**

STEP 5

Layer the pieces as shown, taking care to place the sewn leaf section between the fabric layers. **FIGURE E**

STEP 6

Pin and sew around all layers. Leave an opening in the bottom to turn the hot pad right side out. Clip the corners and turn right side out. Press and edgestitch (page 22) the bottom to close the opening.

You're finished!

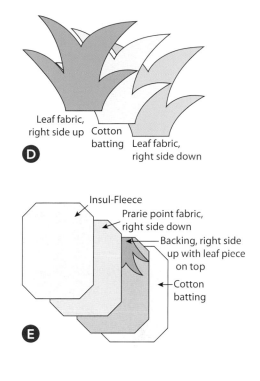

Leaf fabric, right side up   Cotton batting   Leaf fabric, right side down

D

Insul-Fleece
Prarie point fabric, right side down
Backing, right side up with leaf piece on top
Cotton batting

E

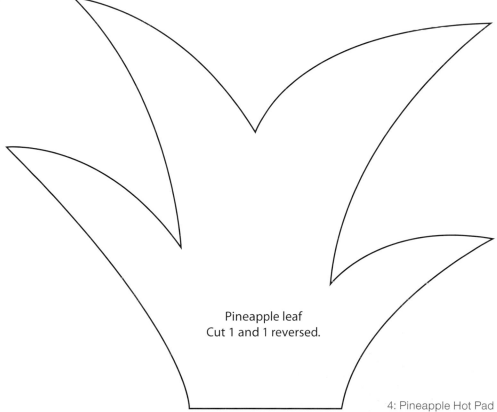

Pineapple leaf
Cut 1 and 1 reversed.

Don't let clutter overwhelm you. Stitch up one of the cute projects in this chapter and you'll have plenty of perfect spaces for just about everything! Storage totes and stylish bins with tassels, as well as a family calendar and office organization (complete with washi tape storage!) make up the projects in this chapter.

September

S M T W T F S

5: Storage and Organization

Laundry Tote

FINISHED SIZE: 20″ in diameter × 18¼″ high

Materials and Supplies

- 7¼″ × 12″ rectangle each of 12 different coordinating fabrics

- 1⅛ yards of main fabric, 42″ wide, for the bottom band and tote base

- 1¾ yards of lining fabric, 42″ wide

- 2 yards of interfacing, 20″ wide (I used Pellon SF101.)

- 2 yards of Timtex interfacing, 20″–22″ wide

- 21″-diameter circle of Soft and Stable stabilizer

- 2 yards of extra-wide double-fold bias binding

- Fabric marking pen

Cutting

From main fabric:

Cut 2 strips 8½″ × 33½″.

Cut a circle 21″ in diameter.

From lining:

Cut 2 rectangles 18¾″ × 33½″.

Cut a circle 21″ in diameter.

From interfacing:

Cut 2 rectangles 18¾″ × 33½″.

Construction

All seams are ¼″ unless noted otherwise.

STEP 1

Mark a straight line from the upper right corner to the lower left corner on the wrong side of each 7¼″ × 12″ rectangle. Pair 2 rectangles right sides together, matching the marked lines. Stitch ¼″ from each side of the marked line.

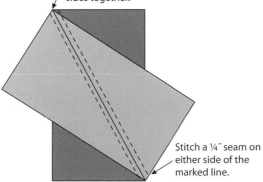

Match the marked lines with the rectangles right sides together.

Stitch a ¼″ seam on either side of the marked line.

Who says that laundry baskets can't look stylish? Don't need a laundry tote? This storage works equally well for extra blankets, magazine collections, or piled shoes by the door!

Techniques Learned/Practiced

- **Making half-rectangle triangles**

- **Insetting a round bottom**

Cut the rectangles on the marked line, press the seams open, and trim each to 6½˝ × 10¾˝. **FIGURE A**

Piece 11 rectangles together into a long strip.

STEP 2

Sew the 2 strips of main fabric together along the short ends to make a long strip. Attach this strip to the bottom of the rectangle strip. **FIGURE B**

STEP 3

Measure the unit from Step 2, subtract ¾˝ from the height and width, and cut a rectangle of Timtex interfacing to this size. Center and iron the Timtex onto the back of the pieced unit, leaving ⅜˝ uncovered on all 4 edges. With right sides together, align and stitch the side edges together to make a large loop. This is the exterior of the tote. Set aside.

STEP 4

Iron the interfacing rectangles to the back of the lining rectangles. Stitch the side edges together to make a large loop.

STEP 5

Place the lining loop inside the exterior loop with right sides together, matching the side seams. Stitch a ½˝ seam along the top edge. **FIGURE C**

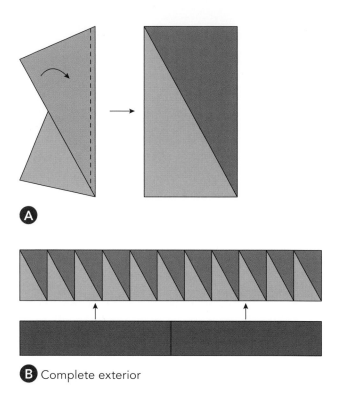

A

B Complete exterior

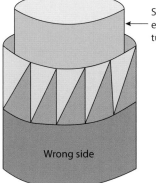

Slide the lining inside the exterior that's been turned inside out.

Wrong side

C Attaching exterior and lining

Press the seam open. Turn the unit right side out, with the right side of the lining on the outside. Press all seams well. Topstitch ¼″ from the top edge. **FIGURE D**

STEP 6

Arrange the main fabric circle and the lining circle, both right side out, with the Soft and Stable circle between them. Baste around the edge. Starting in the center, use a walking foot on your machine to stitch a loose spiral to hold all the layers together. This is the tote bottom. **FIGURE E**

STEP 7

Fold the circle from Step 6 in half horizontally and vertically. Mark the folds on the edge of the circle. Unfold.

STEP 8

With the tote top still inside out, fold the tote top vertically in half; half again, and mark the folds in the seam allowance of the raw edge.

Pin the tote bottom to the raw edges of the tote top, matching the quarter markings and making sure the exterior fabric for the bottom is matched with the exterior fabric for the top. Pin well. Stitch with a ½″ seam.

STEP 9

Cover the raw edge around the inside bottom of the tote by unfolding the bias tape, inserting the raw edge inside, refolding the tape, and stitching the tape in place with a wide zigzag stitch.

Turn the tote right side out, and enjoy!

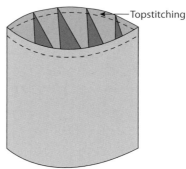

Topstitching

Raw edge of the exterior and lining

D

Quilted spiral

Main fabric, right side up
Soft and Stable stabilizer
Lining fabric, right side down

E Completed tote bottom

Tasseled Storage Bins with Removable Dividers

FINISHED SIZE: Large Bin: 11″ wide × 11″ deep × 8″ high
Small Bin: 7″ wide × 7″ deep × 4″ high • Rectangular Bin: 6″ wide × 13″ deep × 5″ high

Materials and Supplies

For the large bin:

- ⅞ yard of nondirectional medium- to heavyweight fabric, 42″ wide for exterior

- ⅞ yard of nondirectional light- to medium-weight fabric, 42″ wide for lining

- 1⅝ yards of lightweight woven fusible interfacing, 20″ wide

For the small bin:

- ½ yard of nondirectional medium- to heavyweight fabric, 42″ wide for exterior

- ½ yard of nondirectional light- to medium-weight fabric, 42″ wide for lining

- ½ yard of lightweight woven fusible interfacing, 20″ wide

For the rectangular bin:

- ½ yard of nondirectional medium- to heavyweight fabric, 42″ wide for exterior

- ⅝ yard of nondirectional light- to medium-weight fabric, 42″ wide for lining

- ⅞ yard of lightweight woven fusible interfacing, 20″ wide

For all sizes:

- Leather, suede, or vinyl scraps for tassels

- Small/medium tassel caps for each tassel

- Jump ring for each tassel

- E6000 Permanent Craft Adhesive

- Fabric marking pen

- 1 package 72″ × 58″ Soft and Stable stabilizer (This is enough for at least 1 set of bins.)

- 36″ of hook-and-loop tape, ½″ wide

Don't let these sleek storage bins intimidate you. Once you sew up one, you'll be dying to get organized and sew them for every room in your house!

Techniques Learned/Practiced

- Sewing three-dimensional objects

- Making tassels

Cutting

Refer to the table below for cutting directions for each bin.

Storage Bins with Removable Dividers

	Large Bin	Small Bin	Rectangular Bin
Exterior Fabric	Cut 1 square 27″ × 27″, then trim a 7½″ × 7½″ square from each corner.	Cut 1 square 15″ × 15″, then trim a 3½″ × 3½″ square from each corner.	Cut 1 rectangle 16″ × 23″, then trim a 4½″ × 4½″ square from each corner.
Lining and Interfacing	Cut 1 square 28″ × 28″, then trim an 8″ × 8″ square from each corner. Optional dividers: Cut 2 pieces 7″ × 13″.	Cut 1 square 16″ × 16″, then trim a 4″ × 4″ square from each corner.	Cut 1 rectangle 17″ × 24″, then trim a 5″ × 5″ square from each corner. Optional dividers: Cut 4 pieces 4″ × 8″.

STEP 1

Iron the fusible interfacing to the back of the lining.

STEP 2

Place each exterior piece faceup on the stabilizer. Baste all the way around the edge, then cut off the remaining stabilizer.

Note: Since the square for the large bin may be wider than the interfacing, iron interfacing on one half of the lining, and then slightly overlap another piece of interfacing and iron.

Construction

Follow these instructions for all bin sizes. All seams are ½″ unless noted otherwise.

STEP 1

On the bin exterior, align the raw edges of each cut corner, right sides together, and stitch. **FIGURE A**

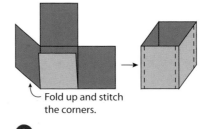

Fold up and stitch the corners.

A

STEP 2

This is an optional step for the large and rectangular bins. If you're not sure you want a divider, you can always add the attachment piece now so you have the option to add dividers later.

Refer to the divider tape placement diagrams (at right) to stitch the divider attachment loop tape in place. Stitch the softer loop side of the hook-and-loop tape to the lining because it will not catch or snag the contents of the bin if you remove the dividers. **FIGURES B & C**

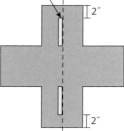

Stitch the tape directly to the left of the centerline.

2″

2″

Divider tape placement: large bin. Use 6″ pieces of hook-and-loop tape.

B Divider tape placement, large bin

STEP 3

Sew the lining corners together, just as you did the exterior in Step 1, *except* leave a small opening along the middle of one side.

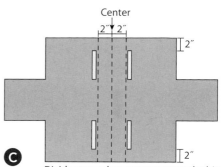

Center

2″ 2″

2″

2″

C Divider tape placement: rectangular bin. Use 3″ pieces of hook-and-loop tape and stitch them to the outside of the 2″ lines.

STEP 4

To make the tassel attachment loop, cut a rectangle of exterior fabric 1¼″ × 3″. If you want pull loops but not tassels, cut a rectangle of exterior fabric 1¼″ × 5″. Fold the rectangle in half lengthwise and press. Unfold, then fold each raw edge in to meet at the first fold. Press, then fold in half again so that all raw edges are enclosed. Stitch a small edge stitch (page 22) down both edges to secure the fold in place. Trim the rectangle to 2½″ long for tassels or 4½″ long for a pull loop only.

Find the center front of the bin. Fold the strip in half to form a loop and baste the raw edges along the top center edge.

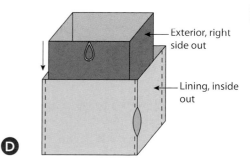

Exterior, right side out

Lining, inside out

D

STEP 5

Place the exterior bin inside the lining, right sides together. Match all 4 corners and pin well. Stitch around all 4 top edges. **FIGURE D**

Turn the bin right side out through the small opening in the lining. Edgestitch (page 22) the lining closed and tuck the lining inside the exterior. The lining is slightly taller than the exterior, so part of the lining will become an accent band across the top of the bin. Press well and stitch in-the-ditch through all layers along the seam where the lining and exterior meet. **FIGURE E**

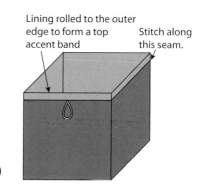

Lining rolled to the outer edge to form a top accent band

Stitch along this seam.

E

STEP 6

(Optional step if you completed Step 2 to add the divider attachments.)

Interface each divider piece with fusible interfacing:

Place the rectangles right sides together, pin, and sew around all 4 edges. Leave a small opening on the bottom for turning. Clip the corners. **FIGURE F**

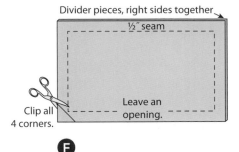

Divider pieces, right sides together.

½˝ seam

Clip all 4 corners.

Leave an opening.

F

Turn right side out, press, and edgestitch (page 22) along both the top and bottom edges. Align the hook pieces of hook-and-loop tape to the side edges of each divider and edgestitch around them. **FIGURE G**

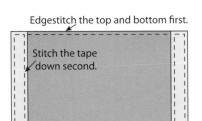

Edgestitch the top and bottom first.

Stitch the tape down second.

G

Slide the divider in place and align with the loop tape in the lining. **FIGURE H**

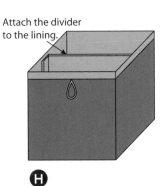

Attach the divider to the lining.

H

STEP 7

To make the tassels, cut a 4˝ × 5˝ rectangle of the leather/suede. Measure the height of the tassel cap. On the back of the leather/suede rectangle, measure this distance from a long edge and draw a line parallel to the long edge. Use sharp scissors to carefully cut ⅛˝ fringe strips up to the marked line. **FIGURE I**

I

Start rolling the top of the rectangle at one end, using the E6000 adhesive as you go to secure it in place. I find it's easiest for me to place the E6000 where I want it by using a toothpick to apply it. Continue rolling until the end of the tassel is just large enough to fit into the tassel cap. Trim off any extra suede. Let dry. Then use the E6000 to secure the tassel inside the cap. **FIGURE J**

Open the jump ring. Attach it to the top of the tassel cap and then to the storage bin loop. If you made the tassel for the small bin, trim it to a shorter length. You're finished!

J Tassel caps can vary in size, finish, and style.

Family
Organizational Chart

FINISHED SIZE: 18″ × 24″

This organizational chart will help keep life on track and all the important dates in one spot. It's magnetic and works as a dry-erase board too!

Techniques Learned/Practiced

- **Proper piecing**

Materials and Supplies

- ⅞ yard of main fabric, 42″ wide
- ¾ yard of white kraft•tex (C&T Publishing), 19″ wide
- 1 fat quarter of coordinating fabric for an erasing cloth
- 18″ × 24″ white frame
- Magnetic metal sheet at least 18″ × 24″ (Usually I use roof flashing from the hardware store.)
- Tin snips
- Small microfiber towel at least 7″ × 7″
- Fabric marking pen
- 31 small neodymium magnets (Other magnets will not hold well through the glass.)
- E6000 Permanent Craft Adhesive
- Glue gun and glue sticks
- 31 small wood disks (Paint if desired.)
- Small number stickers for dates (These should fit on the small wooden disks.)
- Medium-sized (¾″–1″) alphabet stickers for days of the week
- Dry-erase markers

Cutting and Construction

All seams are ½″ unless noted otherwise.

From main fabric:

Cut 1 rectangle 22″ × 28″.

From white kraft•tex:

Cut 1 rectangle 11¼″ × 19¼″.

Cut 1 rectangle 3″ × 10″.

STEP 1

Lay the large main fabric rectangle right side up on a flat surface. Draw a line 3½″ from the bottom. Center the large kraft•tex rectangle on top, aligning the bottom with the marked line. Zigzag around the outer edge of the kraft•tex to secure it in place.

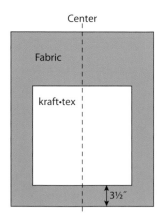

STEP 2

Refer to the marking diagram (below) and use the fabric marking pen to mark lines as shown on the white kraft•tex rectangle. Stitch along these lines with a contrasting thread to divide the rectangle into calendar days. Use the medium-sized alphabet stickers to mark the days of the week on the first row.

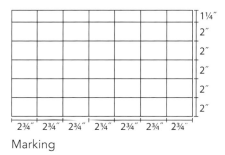

Marking

STEP 3

Mark a horizontal line ¾″ above the calendar grid. Center the small kraft•tex rectangle on the main fabric, aligning the bottom with the marked line. Zigzag around the rectangle to secure in place.

STEP 4

Using the tin snips, carefully cut a piece of metal sheeting 18″ × 24″. It's easiest to mark the lines with a permanent marker, then use the snips to cut along the line. Be careful while using the tin snips and wear heavy gloves to protect your hands. Center the calendar assembly on the metal sheet, wrap the extra fabric around to the back, and use the glue gun to secure in place. Insert the wrapped metal inside the frame, behind the glass.

STEP 5

Affix the number stickers on each of the small wooden disks to make disks for each day of the month, 1–31. Use the E6000 adhesive to attach a magnet to the back of each wooden disk and let dry.

Eraser Construction

Cut a 7″ × 7″ square from the microfiber towel and another 7″ × 7″ square from a fat quarter. Place right sides together and pin. Stitch around the outer edges, leaving a small opening along one side for turning. Clip the corners, turn right side out, and topstitch around all 4 edges to complete the microfiber eraser.

Tip • Design Option: Use a smaller frame and make a weekly menu board instead of a calendar!

SKILL LEVEL

4

The sewing itself isn't challenging, but the cutting and piecing is pretty lengthy.

Hanging Office Storage

FINISHED SIZE: 24″ × 36″

Materials and Supplies

- 1⅓ yards of main fabric, 42″ wide

- ¼ yard of accent fabric 1, 42″ wide (Buy ⅔ yard more if you use the accent fabric to make your own bias binding.)

- ⅓ yard of accent fabric 2, 42″ wide

- ⅓ yard of accent fabric 3, 42″ wide

- 1½ yards of double-fold bias binding, ½″ wide (Use premade binding, or make your own using ⅔ yard extra of accent fabric 1.)

- ¼ yard of coordinating mesh fabric, 48″ wide

- 1 yard of lightweight woven fusible interfacing (such as Pellon SF101), 20″ wide

- 1¼″ × 16″ strip of magnetic metal (Cut from a larger sheet with tin snips if necessary.)

- 1 toggle button, 2″

- 24″ × 36″ rectangle of MDF board, ½″ thick

- Permanent spray adhesive

- 30″ × 42″ rectangle of fusible fleece

- Picture-hanging hardware and appropriate screws/nails to attach it to the back of the board

- Staple gun and staples

- E6000 Permanent Craft Adhesive

Having trouble keeping all the office supplies in one spot? This hanging organizer is the perfect solution! With space for file folders, loops for scissors, washi tape storage, some see-through pockets, and even a magnetic strip, you'll never have to dig for anything important again!

Techniques Learned/Practiced

- **Installing snaps**
- **Sewing with mesh**

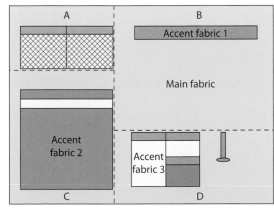

You will work on the organizer in sections, and then sew the sections together at the end.

Cutting

SECTION A

From main fabric:

Cut 1 rectangle 5″ × 11″.

Cut 1 rectangle 14″ × 11″.

From bias binding:

Cut a 14″ length.

From mesh:

Cut 1 rectangle 5½″ × 14″.

SECTION B

From main fabric:

Cut 1 rectangle 3″ × 14″.

Cut 1 rectangle 4″ × 14″.

Cut 1 rectangle 17½″ × 14″.

Cut 1 rectangle 22½″ × 5½″.

From accent fabric 1:

Cut 1 rectangle 17½″ × 4″.

SECTION C

From main fabric:

Cut 1 rectangle 5″ × 18½″.

Cut 1 rectangle 14″ × 10″.

Cut 2 rectangles 14″ × 3½″.

Cut 1 rectangle 14″ × 4½″.

From accent fabric 2, interfaced with SF101:

Cut 2 rectangles 14″ × 9″.

From accent fabric 3, interfaced with SF101:

Cut 1 rectangle 14″ × 9″.

SECTION D

From bias binding:

Cut a length 34″.

From main fabric:

Cut 1 rectangle 3″ × 11″.

Cut 2 rectangles 6½″ × 7″.

Cut 1 rectangle 12″ × 5″.

Cut 1 square 10″ × 10″.

From accent fabric 2, interfaced with SF101:

Cut 1 rectangle 4″ × 6½″.

From accent fabric 3, interfaced with SF101:

Cut 2 rectangles 6¼″ × 6½″.

Construction

All seams are ½″ unless noted otherwise.

Section A

STEP 1

Unfold the double-fold bias binding, insert a long edge of the mesh inside, refold the binding, pin, and stitch. **FIGURE A**

STEP 2

Place the mesh pocket on top of the 14″ × 11″ main fabric rectangle, bottom edges aligned. Baste the bottom and side edges. Stitch down the center to divide the pocket. **FIGURE B**

STEP 3

Stitch the 5″ × 11″ main fabric rectangle to the left of the pocket unit. Press all seams, taking care not to burn or melt the mesh. Set aside. **FIGURE C**

Section B

STEP 1

Fold the accent fabric 1 rectangle in half length-wise, wrong sides together. Center the magnetic metal strip inside, against the fold. Use glue dots to glue baste the edges in place and to hold the metal away from your sewing line. **FIGURE D**

STEP 2

Align the raw edges of the folded magnetic strip with the top edge of the 17½″ × 14″ main fabric rectangle. Pin. Stitch the 3″ × 14″ and 4″ × 14″ main fabric rectangles in place as shown. **FIGURE E**

Stitch the 5½″ × 22½″ main fabric rectangle to the top of the unit to complete Section B. Set aside. **FIGURE F**

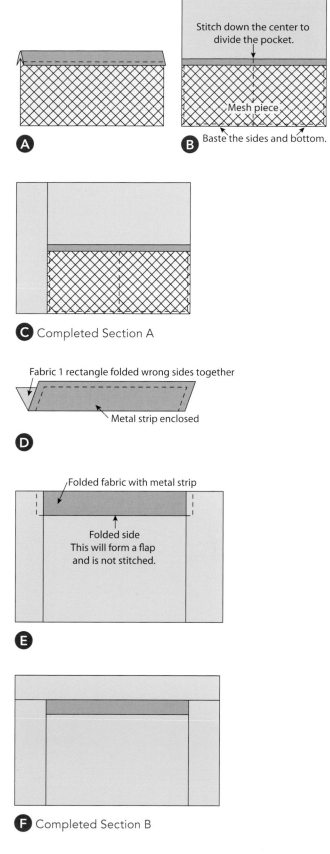

A

B Stitch down the center to divide the pocket. Mesh piece. Baste the sides and bottom.

C Completed Section A

Fabric 1 rectangle folded wrong sides together
Metal strip enclosed
D

Folded fabric with metal strip
Folded side
This will form a flap and is not stitched.
E

F Completed Section B

Section C

STEP 1

To make the pockets from accent fabrics 2 and 3, start by making a ½" double-fold hem (page 23) on one long edge only of all 3 accent fabric rectangles. The hemmed edge will be the top of each pocket.

With right sides together, align the top long edge of a 14" × 3½" main fabric rectangle with the bottom long edge of a 14" × 10" main fabric rectangle. Insert the bottom of an accent fabric 2 pocket between the 2 rectangles, aligning the raw edges. Pin and stitch. Set aside. **FIGURE G**

Place the top long edge of the 14" × 4½" main fabric rectangle, facedown, on the bottom long edge of the remaining 14" × 3½" main fabric piece. Insert the bottom of the remaining fabric 2 pocket. Pin and stitch. **FIGURE H**

Insert the remaining pocket, from accent fabric 3, between the 2 sewn pieces. Pin and stitch. Press well. **FIGURE I**

STEP 2

Press all pockets up and baste both edges. Pin and stitch the 5" × 18½" main fabric rectangle to the left side of the pocket section. Press well and set aside. **FIGURE J**

Section D

STEP 1

Cut a 12" length of bias tape. Topstitch the folded edges together. Thread the toggle button through the bias tape and center it. Overlap the raw edge on top and pin together. Set aside. **FIGURE K**

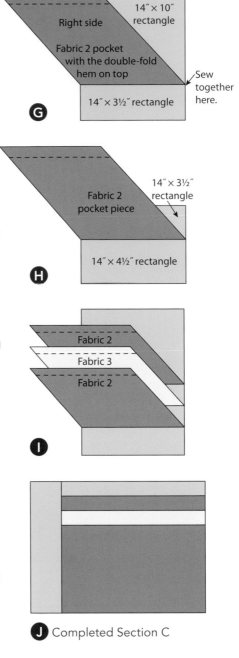

G 14" × 10" rectangle · Right side · Fabric 2 pocket with the double-fold hem on top · 14" × 3½" rectangle · Sew together here.

H Fabric 2 pocket piece · 14" × 3½" rectangle · 14" × 4½" rectangle

I Fabric 2 · Fabric 3 · Fabric 2

J Completed Section C

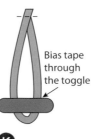

K Bias tape through the toggle

Tip • To use the washi tape storage, fold the toggle button parallel to the bias tape, slide the tape rolls on, then straighten it to hold the washi tape in place.

STEP 2

On the 10″ × 10″ main fabric square, mark the top edge 3¼″ from the left. Place the raw edges of the toggle loop on the mark. Baste and set aside.

STEP 3

Unfold the double-fold bias binding and insert the 6½″ edge of the 4″ × 6½″ accent fabric 2 rectangle. Refold, pin, and stitch. Repeat this process with a 6½″ edge of each of the 6¼″ × 6½″ fabric 3 rectangles.

Refer to the pocket assembly diagram (at right) to layer the pieces in 2 units, with all bottom edges aligned with a 6½″ × 7″ main fabric rectangle, right side up, underneath the accent fabric pieces. Baste the side edges of each unit, then stitch the right and left units together. **FIGURE L**

STEP 4

Stitch the 12″ × 5″ main fabric rectangle to the bottom of the pocket unit. Stitch the 3″ × 11″ main fabric rectangle to the left side and the toggle unit to the right side to complete the section. **FIGURE M**

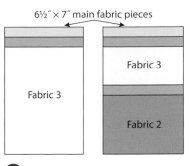

6½″ × 7″ main fabric pieces

Fabric 3

Fabric 3

Fabric 2

L Pocket assembly

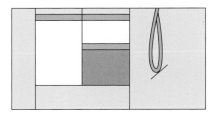

M Completed Section D

Finishing Up

STEP 1

Piece Sections A and C together and Sections B and D together. Stitch the units together along the vertical seam to complete the top.

STEP 2

Iron the fusible fleece to the back of this main section and trim away the extra fleece. Spray the MDF board with the permanent spray adhesive and place the completed organizer on top. Make sure you press down to adhere the organizer well.

STEP 3

Working from the back, wrap all raw edges around to the back. Use a staple gun to secure the fabric to the board.

STEP 4

Add proper hanging hardware and hang!

6
Walls, Floors, and Decor

Ready to add variety to your space with some fun accent projects? Learn how to turn a favorite fabric into a perfect entry rug, how to easily make new throw pillows, and much more.

110

116

DIY Rug

FINISHED SIZE: 24″ × 36″

Materials and Supplies

- 24″ × 36″ rectangle of Roc-lon multipurpose cloth (see Resources, page 143)

- Large paintbrush

- 1 yard of feature fabric—lightweight quilting cotton or medium-weight printed home decor canvas

- 11′ of twill tape, 1½″ wide

- Clear water-based polyacrylic, satin finish

- Mod Podge Matte

- Foam craft brush

- Clear silicone sealant/caulk

Note: Multipurpose cloth is great for this project because it doesn't need to be primed, doesn't fray when cut, and is extremely durable. Use it for rugs, as an art canvas, or even as drapery lining.

Cutting

From feature fabric:

Cut a rectangle 28″ × 40″.

Note: If your fabric has a large repeat or a center medallion, make sure it is centered. Find the center, then measure out from there to find the cut lines. See Cutting Fabric with Large Repeats (page 18).

Learn just how easy it is to take a favorite fabric and make a perfect entry rug that's also easily cleaned! No need to worry about muddy feet or pets getting it dirty. The polyacrylic finish means it is easy to wipe clean and back into pristine condition in no time!

Techniques Learned/Practiced

- **Working with polyacrylic**

Construction

STEP 1

Working on a surface that's protected with a painter's drop cloth or plastic tarp, apply Mod Podge to the multipurpose cloth and adhere the feature fabric to the cloth. Work in small 10″-square sections, applying it a little at a time. Take care to center the fabric on the multipurpose cloth. Let dry.

STEP 2

When the fabric is dry, turn the piece over. Fold all 4 corners in at an angle and adhere them to the back of the mat with the Mod Podge.

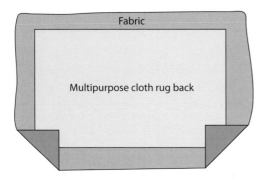

Next, fold the 4 edges of the feature fabric in and adhere them to the back of the mat. Let dry.

STEP 3

Still working over the protected surface, cover the entire front of the rug with a layer of polyacrylic clear sealer. Let the mat dry for the time suggested on the sealer container. Add another coat and let dry.

Flip the mat to the back and seal the back and edges of the rug as well. Let the sealer completely set and cure for approximately 48 hours. To finish the raw edges, use an epoxy glue to cover them with the twill tape.

To make a nonskid backing, use clear silicone to make multiple lines across the entire back. You're finished!

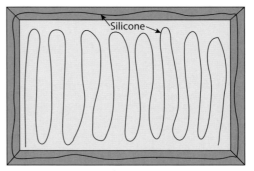

Keep the silicone lines no more than several inches apart.

Corded Throw Pillow

FINISHED SIZE: 19″ × 19″

Throw pillows
are a simple and
quick way to up-
date your space!

Techniques Learned/Practiced

- Making and applying pillow cording

- Inserting a regular zipper

Materials and Supplies

- ⅔ yard of feature fabric, 42˝ wide

- 3 yards of cording, ¹²∕₃₂˝ diameter

- 3 yards of a bias-cut strip, 2½˝ wide (may be pieced from shorter strips) to cover cording

- 20˝ pillow form

- 22˝ regular zipper in a coordinating color

- 1⅓ yards of Pellon SF101 (optional for medium- or heavyweight fabrics but necessary for lightweight fabric)

Tip • Consider choosing a more budget-friendly fabric for the pillow back to allow extra money for a stand-out front fabric! You'll still need the full ⅔ yard for the front, but you'll be able to make 2 pillows from it.

Note: A note about pillow forms: A large variety of pillow forms are available. I prefer a down or down-alternative pillow form. The down pillows are more cushy and look more natural than a stiff, polyfill pillow form. You also can choose allergy-free down alternatives that have the same look but don't use real down.

Cutting

From feature fabric:

Cut 1 square 20˝ × 20˝ for the front.

Cut 1 rectangle 3½˝ × 20˝ and 1 rectangle 17½˝ × 20˝ for the back.

Tip • If you are using a lightweight fabric, back it with a woven interfacing.

Construction

All seams are ½˝ unless noted otherwise.

STEP 1

Insert a standard zipper (page 25) between the 20˝ edges of the backing rectangles.

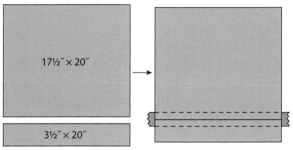

17½˝ × 20˝

3½˝ × 20˝

Pillow back with zipper

STEP 2

Make and attach cording (page 22) to the outer edge of the pillow front.

STEP 3

Open the zipper halfway. Place the front and back pieces right sides together, aligning all edges. Stitch around the perimeter of the pillow cover, backstitching over the seam where the zipper ends are. Clip the corners and trim any extra zipper that extends past the backing. Turn right side out through the zippered opening.

STEP 4

Stuff the pillow with the pillow form and zip it up.

Tip • I prefer the look of a pillow cover that's slightly smaller than the pillow form. This ensures a pillow that looks nice, full, and fluffy.

Knife–Edge Throw Pillow

FINISHED SIZE: 14˝ × 24˝

Materials and Supplies

- 8 fabric scraps in various sizes ranging from 6″ to 15″ square

- ½ yard of coordinating fabric for pillow back

- 24″ concealed zipper in a coordinating color

- 14″ × 24″ pillow form

- 1½ yards of Pellon SF101 (optional for lightweight fabric)

- Corner template (page 118)

Note: The corner template is essential to getting a finished designer look with a knife-edge pillow. It may seem counterintuitive to shape the edges of a square pillow, but when it's completely sewn up, you'll see the difference. The shaping keeps the corners from turning into ears and pointing outward, losing the shape of your crisp, square knife-edge pillow.

Cutting

The cut sizes are listed width × height as the pieces appear in the pillow to help you plan any directional fabric accordingly.

From scraps:

Cut 1 each of the following:

A: 4″ × 14″	E: 5¼″ × 9″
B: 4″ × 5¼″	F: 12¾″ × 5½″
C: 4″ × 9¼″	G: 4¾″ × 9¼″
D: 8″ × 9″	H: 4¾″ × 5¼″

From coordinating fabric:

Cut 1 rectangle 14″ × 24″

Note: This particular pillow front is pieced for a contemporary look. To make the project even easier, use 2 rectangles of fabric cut 14″ × 24″ and start at Step 2.

My favorite quick pillow project uses two same-sized rectangles (or squares) and a concealed zipper. Don't let a concealed zipper intimidate you. Once you put one in, you'll ask yourself, "Why haven't I done this before?"

Techniques Learned/Practiced

- Making a knife-edge with a professional corner

- Inserting a concealed zipper

Construction

All seams are ½″ unless noted otherwise.

STEP 1

Piece together the pillow front with ¼″ seams, referring to the piecing diagram for block placement. Press the seams open as you go so they'll lie flat. Add interfacing if desired.

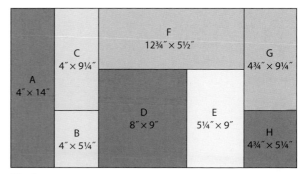

Piecing

STEP 2

Trace the corner pattern onto paper or plastic to make a template. Align the corner template as shown and trim the corners of the front and back.

STEP 3

Insert the concealed zipper in one long edge (see Concealed Zipper, page 25). Open the zipper about halfway. Sew around the remaining 3 edges of the pillow with a regular or walking foot. Turn the pillow cover right side out, insert the pillow form, zip up, and enjoy!

Tip • Design Option: Since the zipper is hidden on the bottom, consider making the pillow reversible! Change out the back for a coordinating fabric, or use a different color scheme altogether!

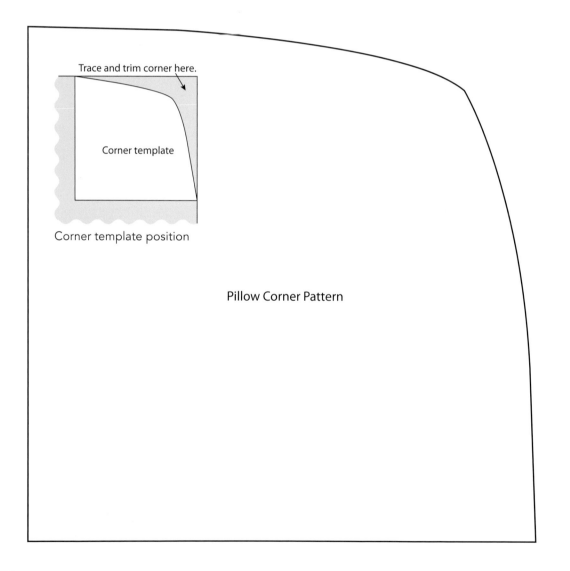

Trace and trim corner here.

Corner template

Corner template position

Pillow Corner Pattern

SKILL LEVEL

Art Clock

FINISHED SIZE: 20˝ in diameter

I love a functional art piece. This clock is the perfect way to use a favorite fabric and make a decor piece for the wall.

Materials and Supplies

- ¾ yard of light- to medium-weight feature fabric
- ½ yard of white kraft•tex, 19″ wide (C&T Publishing)
- 2 sheets of card stock for your printer
- 20″-round artist canvas
- Rust-Oleum gold spray paint
- Clock kit with 4″–5″ hands
- Permanent spray adhesive
- Removable fabric marking pen
- Glue gun and glue sticks
- Staple gun and staples
- E6000 Permanent Craft Adhesive
- Precision scissors or craft knife
- Picture-hanging hardware

Cutting and Construction

STEP 1

Paint the white kraft•tex with the gold spray paint. Let dry. Paint the clock hands with gold spray paint as well.

STEP 2

Using a computer, print out the roman numerals 1–12 (I–XII). Choose a narrow sans serif font like Arial or Century Gothic. Choose a size that will print out approximately 3″ tall. Print the numbers on thick card stock.

Cut out all the symbols with precision scissors or a craft knife. When the painted kraft•tex fabric is dry, trace all the numerals onto it and carefully cut them out. Set aside.

STEP 3

Find the center of the feature fabric by folding it in half horizontally and then vertically, lightly pressing the folded edges. Use a compass and removable fabric marker to draw a circle with a 6″ radius, starting at the center point. Arrange the numerals, aligning the bottom of the letters with the drawn circle. Use the glue gun to affix the symbols in place to make the clock face.

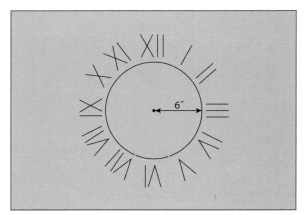

Numeral alignment

STEP 4

Cut a small hole in the center of the canvas and the center of the clock face. The hole should be just a little smaller than the clock mechanism post. The canvas and fabric will stretch slightly, so it's better for the hole to be too small instead of too big.

STEP 5

Use the spray adhesive to fully coat the top and sides of the canvas. Starting in the center, with the center holes aligned, adhere the fabric clock front to the canvas. Wrap the fabric tightly around the edges of the canvas. Trim off the extra fabric, leaving a 2″ margin.

STEP 6

Wrap the 2″ of extra fabric to the back of the canvas and secure with a staple gun. Following the instructions that came with the clock mechanism, insert the clock mechanism on the back and the hands on the front. Secure the mechanism in the back with epoxy glue and let it set for 1 or 2 days.

Although there's probably a hanging hook on the mechanism itself, attach hanging hardware to the top of the canvas frame back. This will hold the clock better than the one on the mechanism. After it's dry, hang it in your favorite spot!

Pendant Light Shade

FINISHED SIZE: 23" in diameter × 14" tall

Materials and Supplies

- 1 drum lamp shade, 23″ in diameter × 14″ tall
- 1⅛ yards of feature fabric
- Spray adhesive
- Masking tape or painter's tape
- Hot glue gun and extra glue sticks
- Small-tipped scissors that have a sharp point

Cutting

From feature fabric:

Cut 2 rectangles 16″ × 38″.

Construction

STEP 1

Place the fabric rectangles horizontally in front of you. On the right-hand side of each rectangle, fold and stitch a ¼″ double-fold hem (page 23).

STEP 2

Tape off the metal frame of the lamp shade with painter's tape or masking tape to protect it from the adhesive. On a protected surface, in a space with good ventilation, attach one of the fabric rectangles to the lamp shade using the spray adhesive. Centering the rectangle vertically on the lamp shade, start with the unhemmed short edge and work your way around to the double-fold hem. The fabric will go about halfway around the lamp shade and should hang over the lamp shade about 1″ at the top and bottom. At the end, leave about 1″ of the hemmed edge unattached.

Slide the unhemmed short edge of the second fabric rectangle under the hemmed edge of the first and continue using the spray adhesive to cover the lamp shade with the fabric.

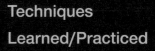

Overlap hemmed edge over raw edge of other piece.

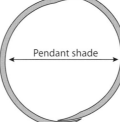

Pendant shade

View from the top of the pendant

Techniques Learned/Practiced

- **Working with spray adhesive**
- **Making a double-fold hem**

STEP 3

Use a very small amount of hot glue to adhere the hemmed edges to the front of the lamp shade. Then apply a small line of glue to the inside top of the frame, fold over the fabric overhang, and adhere. Repeat the process with the bottom overhang.

STEP 4

Finish the inside edge by trimming off all extra fabric at the top and bottom edges. You're finished!

7
Outdoor Sewing

Not only can you sew for all your indoor spaces, but with the proper outdoor fabric, pillow and cushion inserts, and the right thread, it's entirely possible to create an inviting and livable outdoor space.

The projects in this chapter will introduce you to all the proper techniques for sewing projects to decorate your outdoor living space! Don't forget that you can adapt projects in earlier sections, such as the Knife-Edge Pillow (page 116) or Color-Blocked Place Mats (page 80), for outdoor use by choosing the appropriate materials. To help you know what works and what won't in any outdoor sewing project, see Choosing Materials for the Outdoors (next page).

126

129

133

137

140

This is my HAPPY place.

Choosing Materials for the Outdoors

Outdoor Fabrics

Not just any fabric will work for your outdoor space. Outdoor fabrics are specially designed to withstand wide temperature variations, sun, and rain. You may spend a little more for these fabrics because of their durability. Look for fabrics that specifically say they are for outdoor use. While these fabrics used to be difficult to find, they are now easier to find at large home decor fabric stores as well as online.

Always remember that they are still fabrics; if your projects are not going to be used for a while (such as over the winter or while you are on vacation), bring them inside to preserve them for the next season!

Appropriate Outdoor Inserts

As much as I love the look of down pillow inserts, they are best left indoors. Several varieties of pillow and cushion inserts are available for outdoor use. Look for cushions, outdoor batting, and pillow inserts specifically labeled for outdoor use. These are designed to provide a nice shape and are porous enough to dry quickly if wet. Some are specially treated to resist mold and mildew.

Thread

Typically cotton and polyester threads are not designed to withstand the abuse they will get outdoors. Look for thread that is specifically made for outdoor use. This thread is generally made from a synthetic material that makes it durable in sun and rain. It is usually thick, so you may need a larger needle.

Note: If you are making an item for an outdoor space such as a covered or enclosed patio that doesn't get much direct sun and typically stays dry, you could use a cotton canvas in place of an outdoor fabric. Use thread and inserts designed for outdoor projects, and treat your completed item with a waterproofing spray—just to add some extra protection.

Gusseted Cushion with Lap Zipper

— FINISHED SIZE: 21″ wide × 21″ deep × 4″ high —

Materials and Supplies

- 1½ yards of outdoor main fabric, 54″ wide

- 1 yard of outdoor accent fabric for contrasting cording

- 6 yards of clear plastic tubing, ¼″ diameter

- A dowel rod cut into 2 lengths 1″ each, ³⁄₁₆″ diameter

- 22″ × 22″ square of Nu-Foam outdoor-use cushion material, 4″ thick

- 22″ heavy-duty polyester zipper

- Coordinating thread for outdoor use

Note: The zipper teeth in the heavy-duty zipper for outdoor use *cannot* be shortened easily, so be sure to use a zipper that's the exact length.

Cutting

From main fabric:

Cut 2 squares 23″ × 23″ for top and bottom.

Cut 3 rectangles 5″ × 22″ for side gusset.

Cut 2 rectangles 3″ × 22″ for zippered side of gusset.

Note: The side pieces are cut slightly shorter than the top and bottom. This is to take into account that the cording will curve around the corners.

Construction

All seams are ½″ unless noted otherwise.

STEP 1

Make 2 sections of cording each 8′ long (see Cording, page 22) using the small plastic tubing instead of cotton cording. The tubing will be more durable in an outdoor environment.

This cushion is so wonderful that you will want to keep it out year-round. But the gusset and zipper make it easy for you to switch out different covers, or the inserts, if one wears out before the other.

Techniques Learned/Practiced

- Inserting a regular zipper

- Making and applying cording

STEP 2

Baste the completed cording to the right sides of the top and bottom cushion squares. Curve the cording around the corners slightly, keeping the raw edge of the cording aligned with the raw edges of the straight sides. **FIGURE A**

To secure the 2 ends of the plastic tubing, cut a 1″ length of the ³⁄₁₆″ dowel rod. Insert half into one end of the tubing, and the other half into the opposite end of the tubing. **FIGURE B**

STEP 3

Attach a standard zipper (see Standard Zipper, page 25) between the 3″ × 22″ gusset rectangles.

STEP 4

Stitch the zippered gusset and the 3 side gusset rectangles together end-to-end, leaving ½″ unstitched at the top and bottom of each seam; backstitch at each end of the seams. **FIGURE C**

STEP 5

To complete the cushion, align each side gusset seam with a corner of the cushion top. Place the zippered gusset at the back of the cushion, with the zipper open about halfway. Pin each corner and align the side seams in place. Continue pinning all 4 edges, then stitch the gusset to the cushion top, using a narrow zipper foot or cording foot to sew along the edge of the fabric and cording. **FIGURE D**

STEP 6

Use the same method to pin and stitch the bottom cushion square to the remaining edge of the side gusset. Open the zipper *all the way* and turn the cushion cover right side out.

STEP 7

Stuff the piece of foam inside the cushion. Zip up the cushion cover and place it on the chair!

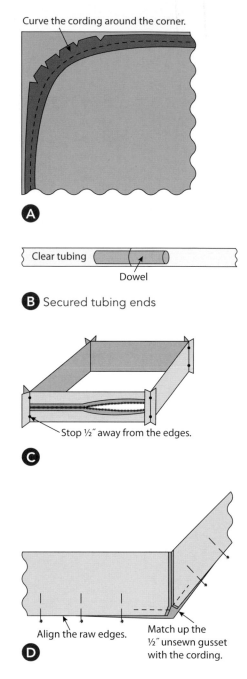

Curve the cording around the corner.

A

Clear tubing

Dowel

B Secured tubing ends

Stop ½″ away from the edges.

C

Align the raw edges.

Match up the ½″ unsewn gusset with the cording.

D

Lemon Slice Picnic Blanket

FINISHED SIZE: 80″ diameter

Quilted by Joanna Marsh
of Kustom Kwilts

Picnic in style with this super cute and refreshing lemon slice picnic blanket, complete with water-resistant laminated backing.

Techniques Learned/Practiced

• Appliquéing

• Sewing with laminated cotton

Materials and Supplies

• 5 yards of laminated cotton, 42″ wide

• 7⅓ yards of main yellow fabric, 42″ wide, cut into 1 length 5 yards and 1 length 2⅓ yards

• 4 yards of white fabric, 42″ wide

• 1 yard of striped fabric, 42″ wide, for binding

• Double-size low-loft batting

• Fabric marking pen

• 2 cans of repositionable fabric spray adhesive

• Washable glue

Cutting

From the 2⅓-yard length of yellow fabric:

Cut 6 rectangles 17″ × 27″.

Fold 1 rectangle in half lengthwise and press lightly on the fold. On the raw-edge side, measure and mark 7¾″ from one end. Draw an arc from the mark to the opposite corner of the fold. Next, draw a diagonal line from the mark to the opposite folded corner to make a teardrop-shaped piece. Cut along the drawn line. Repeat this step with the remaining yellow rectangles. Set aside.

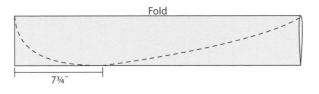

Fold

7¾″

With the 4-yard length of white fabric:

Fold the fabric in half horizontally and cut to make 2 lengths of 2 yards each. Trim off the selvages and piece along the long edges to make a large rectangle approximately 72″ × 81″. Press the seam open. Fold in half horizontally, then vertically, to make a quarter-folded piece.

From the folded corner, measure and mark 35″ on each folded edge.

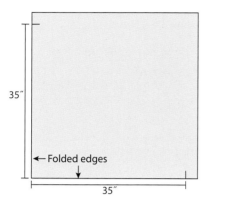

Create a 35″ arc shape by measuring from the point and making a mark every couple of inches.

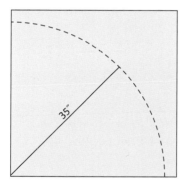

Cut along the marks and unfold the fabric into a large circle. Place a mark on the center point of the circle with the fabric marking pen, then press well.

From the binding fabric:

Cut enough 2¼″ bias binding strips to total 260″. Sew them end-to-end into a long strip.

Construction

STEP 1

Working on a clean, flat surface, lay out the large white circle and then place the 6 yellow wedges as shown. Remember that all fruits are organic in nature and won't be perfectly shaped. Don't worry too much if you can't get all 6 wedges perfectly aligned; just do the best you can!

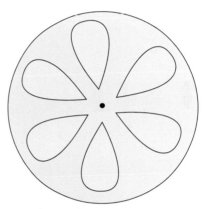

Use the marked center point as a guide to arrange the wedges.

Spray the fabric adhesive on the back of each wedge shape, one at a time, and place it back on the large circle.

Tip • I typically use a painter's drop cloth laid out in the garage or on the patio to keep the overspray mess to a minimum.

Using an appliqué stitch, stitch around the edge of each yellow wedge shape.

STEP 2

Cut the 5 yards of yellow fabric in half horizontally to make 2 lengths 2½ yards each. Trim off the selvages and piece along the long edges to make 1 large rectangle approximately 81″ × 90″. Press the seam open. Find the middle of this piece and align the middle mark of the circle with the middle of this fabric. Use the spray adhesive to adhere the white circle on top of the yellow rectangle. Using an appliqué stitch, stitch around the edge of the white circle.

STEP 3

Cut the 5 yards of laminated cotton in half horizontally to make 2 lengths 2½ yards each. Trim off the selvages and piece the long edges to make a large rectangle approximately 81″ × 90″.

Tip • *Because you are sewing right sides together, you can use a standard walking foot; no need for a specialty nonstick foot.*

STEP 4

Make a quilt sandwich:

First, lay out the laminated cotton, right side down, and spray it with a quilt basting spray. Place the low-loft batting on top, taking care to smooth out any wrinkles. Spray the batting with adhesive and place the appliquéd rectangle on top, right side up.

Note: Typically I would pin baste all layers together to prepare for quilting. But pin marks won't come out of the laminated cotton, so it's better to use the basting spray for this step.

STEP 5

Use a walking foot or free-motion quilting foot to quilt through all layers. The quilting is up to you. It can be dense or loose; just check the recommendations of the batting you purchased for guidelines on how far apart to space the quilting lines.

STEP 6

Around the outer edge of the white circle, measure and mark an outer circle 5″ from the edge. Trim on this line through all layers to make the quilt a large circle.

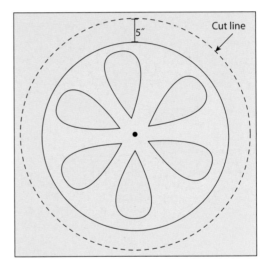

STEP 7

Sew the binding strip to the wrong side of the quilt, using a ¼″ seam. Flip the binding over to the front of the quilt and glue baste it in place with the washable glue. Stitch a wide zigzag around the edge of the binding to secure in place. You're finished!

Cushion, Pillow, and Accessory Pocket for Premade Hammock

FINISHED SIZE: Cushion: 53″ × 77″ • Pillow: 19″ × 11″ • Pocket: 10″ × 12″

Relax in style with this custom hammock cushion. This cushion will fit on most double hammocks that are 55″ × 78″ in size. Make the cushion, pillow, and snack/magazine pocket, then easily attach them to the hammock. Hang the hammock from a tree or a hammock stand and enjoy the afternoon breeze!

Techniques Learned/Practiced

- Working with outdoor fabrics

Materials and Supplies

- Premade double-size hammock
- 5¼ yards of outdoor fabric, 54″ wide, for the main fabric and the pocket
- ½ yard of accent fabric for the pillow
- 12″ × 20″ outdoor pillow insert
- 56″ × 80″ piece of high-loft polyester batting, ¾″–1″ thick
- 20″ concealed zipper
- Coordinating outdoor thread

Cutting

From main fabric:

Cut 2 rectangles 54″ × 78″ for cushion.

Cut 2 rectangles 11″ × 23″ for pocket.

Cut 6 strips 2″ × width of fabric for cushion and pocket ties.

From accent fabric:

Cut 2 rectangles 12″ × 20″ for pillow.

Cut 1 strip 2″ × width of fabric for pillow ties.

From high-loft batting:

Cut 1 rectangle 54″ × 78″.

Construction

All seams are ½˝ unless noted otherwise.

Pillow

STEP 1

To make the ties from both fabrics, start by folding a 2˝ strip in half lengthwise. Press. Unfold, then fold each long edge in toward the center pressed line. Press. Fold each edge again toward the center and press. Topstitch along the folded edges to close the tie. Cut the tie in half lengthwise.

Use the same method to fold and stitch the remaining 2˝ strips to make a total of 14 ties. Set aside.

STEP 2

Place a 12˝ × 20˝ accent fabric rectangle on a flat surface, right side up. On a 20˝ side, mark 2˝ from each corner. Fold 2 accent fabric ties in half and place the folded edges at the marks, against the raw edge of the fabric. Pin in place, then baste.

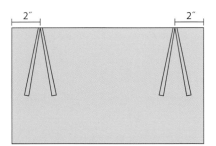

Pillow tie placement

Place the remaining 12˝ × 20˝ rectangle on top, right side down. Insert a concealed zipper (page 25) opposite the side with the basted ties.

Open the zipper about halfway. Sew around the remaining 3 edges. Turn the pillow cover right side out, insert the outdoor pillow form, zip up, and set aside.

Pocket

STEP 1

Place an 11˝ × 23˝ main fabric rectangle faceup on a flat surface. On an 11˝ side, mark 1˝ from each corner. Fold 2 ties in half and place the folded edges at the marks, against the raw edge of the fabric. Pin in place, then baste.

Pocket tie placement

STEP 2

Place the remaining 11″ × 23″ rectangle on top, right side down. Stitch around all edges, leaving a 5″ opening along the short edge opposite the ties.

Turn right side out and press the entire pocket well. Topstitch the bottom edge to secure the opening.

STEP 3

Fold up 10″ from the bottom edge and press. Edgestitch along both side edges to form the pocket. Set aside.

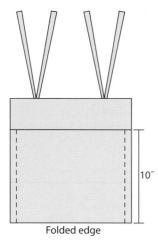

Folded edge

Finished pocket

Cushion

STEP 1

Place a 54″ × 78″ main fabric rectangle on a flat surface, right side up. Fold the 10 remaining ties in half. Referring to the tie placement diagram (below), pin and baste the ties with the folded edges aligned with the raw edges of the rectangle.

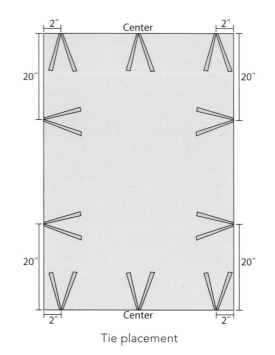

Tie placement

STEP 2

Place the remaining 54″ × 78″ rectangle on top, right side down, followed by the rectangle of high-loft batting. Pin well and stitch around all edges, leaving a 12″–14″ opening along one edge. Turn right side out and topstitch to secure the opening.

STEP 3

Using a walking foot, quilt some vertical lines every 10″–12″ to secure the batting inside the cushion.

Putting It All Together

Tie the cushion to the hammock, followed by the pillow and pocket. Load up the pocket with your favorite magazine and snacks, and you're ready for an afternoon of relaxing!

Waterproof Patio Art

FINISHED SIZE: 14″ × 18″

This
is my
HAPPY
place.

Who says that art can be seen and appreciated only indoors? Use some of your favorite fabrics and complete this no-sew project to admire on the patio all year long!

Techniques Learned/Practiced

- Cutting fabric for appliqué
- Using multipurpose cloth

Required Materials and Supplies

- 14″ × 22″ rectangle of Roc-lon multipurpose cloth (see Resources, page 143)
- Mod Podge Outdoor
- 16″ × 24″ rectangle of neutral background fabric
- Teal and yellow fabric scraps for quote and sun cutouts
- Polyacrylic clear sealer and paintbrush
- E6000 Permanent Craft Adhesive
- A sheet of paper at least 11″ square for the sun pattern and printer paper for the letter patterns
- Heavy starch spray
- Branch (for a more natural, outdoor look) or dowel at least 18″ long, 1″ diameter (or smaller)

Construction

STEP 1

Cover the front of the multipurpose cloth piece with the outdoor Mod Podge. Carefully affix the neutral background fabric to it. Make sure there are no creases or lumps and that everything is nice and smooth. Let it dry, then turn the piece over and fold the extra 1″ of fabric to the back and secure it with more Mod Podge.

STEP 2

While the background is drying, prepare the quote and sun shape.

Cut out a 10″ yellow circle. From the top of the circle, measure down from the top 4″ and trim across to make the sun shape.

Cut various lengths and widths of small yellow strips for the sun rays from the remainder of your yellow circle. Set aside.

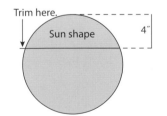

Trim here.

Sun shape

4″

STEP 3

Heavily starch the fabrics for the text and set aside to dry. Use a word processing or photo-editing program to arrange the lettering. Type "This is my" and "place." Adjust the lettering height so the uppercase T is approximately 1¾" high. Print. Use the printout as a pattern to cut your shapes from the teal fabric. Then type "HAPPY" into the program. Adjust the sizing so the uppercase letters are about 2¾" high. Print. Use the printout as a pattern to cut your shapes from the yellow fabric.

STEP 4

Once the background has dried, apply another coat of outdoor Mod Podge to the top of it. This time, though, apply it a little at a time. While it's still wet, affix the letters, sun, and sun rays to it. Let it dry, then coat with another layer of outdoor Mod Podge. Once this has dried, coat with 2 layers of the polyacrylic sealer.

STEP 5

Turn the artwork over and coat the back and edges with the polyacrylic sealer. When the sealer is thoroughly dry, fold the top edge over the branch or dowel to determine how much of a fold you need. Remove the branch and put a bead of E6000 on the top edge of the back. Fold the edge down to the desired length to form a hanging sleeve and place some heavy books along the glued edge to hold it in place while the glue dries.

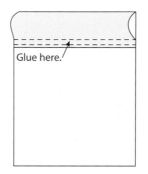

Glue here.

When the glue is dry, insert the branch or dowel into the top and hang!

Tip • If you have a digital die cutter, use it to cut out your fabric letters, easy-peasy!

Sheer Outdoor Patio Drapes

FINISHED PANEL SIZE: 60˝ × 120˝

Materials and Supplies

- 3⅝ yards of 60″-wide outdoor sheer material (For a panel length other than 10′, determine the finished length and add 4″ to calculate how much fabric to buy.)

- 1 yard of main outdoor fabric, 54″ wide

- Coordinating outdoor thread

- Tear-away stabilizer or tracing paper (optional)

Tip • Use a pair of serrated scissors to cut the sheer material. These are specially designed to hold and cut slippery fabrics.

Cutting

From sheer fabric:

Cut the length to 10′4″ (124″).

From main fabric:

Cut 3 strips 6″ × width of fabric. Piece together along the short sides and trim to make 2 strips 61″ long.

Cut 5 strips 2¼″ × width of fabric.

Construction

All seams are ½″ unless noted otherwise.

STEP 1

To make the ties, start by folding a 2¼″ strip in half lengthwise. Press. Unfold, then fold each long edge in toward the center pressed line. Fold the strip in half again so the folded edges meet, and close the long folded edge with an edge stitch (page 22). The folded strip will be about ½″ wide. Cut the strip in half and set aside. Continue this process with the 4 remaining 2¼″ strips. (You will make 10, but you need only 9 for this project.)

Even patios can benefit from drapes. Learn to sew on sheer fabric and add some shade, privacy, and bug protection to your favorite outdoor space!

Techniques Learned/Practiced

- **Sewing with sheers**

STEP 2

Fold the bottom long edge of both 6″ × 61″ main fabric strips up ½″ and press well. Place 1 strip right side up on a flat surface.

Fold each of the 9 ties in half. Starting ⅝″ from each end, align the folded edge of a tie with the top raw edge of the 6″ strip. Continue adding ties 7½″ apart across the top of the strip. Pin and baste in place.

Place the other 6″ × 61″ strip on top, right side down. Stitch around both ends and the top, keeping the bottom folded edges open.

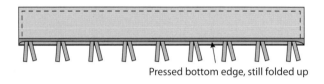

Pressed bottom edge, still folded up

STEP 3

Trim the corners and turn the piece from Step 2 right side out. Press well. Press the ½″ bottom fold again if necessary. Insert the top edge of the sheer fabric 1″ inside the bottom section and pin well. Edgestitch (page 22) to close the bottom edge and secure the sheer to the top fabric panel.

Note: The sheer edges will be left as is. No need to hem them when they're already treated to not fray! If you want to make the next step easier, use premade outdoor sheers and just insert the top edge inside the fabric header. The bottom will already be hemmed!

STEP 4

Use a low setting on the iron to make a 4″ double-fold hem (page 23) on the sheer bottom. Finish with a blind hem (page 24). Use a walking foot if necessary to keep the fabrics from shifting. If you need some extra stabilization, try putting a strip of tear-away stabilizer or tracing paper on the top and bottom of the hem. You'll be able to see through them, and they'll help secure the sheer as you're stitching the hem!

You're finished! Hang outside and enjoy!

About the Author

Erin's love of sewing and design began in elementary school as she graphed the dimensions of her bedroom, which she then proceeded to fill with home decor projects of her own design. By high school she was teaching private sewing lessons and leading DIY projects of all sorts. Afterward, she crisscrossed the country, earning a degree in interior design.

Photo by Heidi Walker, East End Photography

Erin regularly teaches a variety of workshops, guild events, and summer camps, where she never lets anyone give up on their next creative endeavor. Her work has been published in numerous design magazines, and fabric manufacturers and sewing machine companies who appreciate her clean, efficient projects frequently solicit her designs. When she's not teaching classes, Erin enjoys working with her interior design clients, creating her own line of sewing patterns, cooking with her husband, and napping with the cats.

Resources

Hardware, Tools, and Supplies
Drapery hardware, pleat and grommet tape
Rowley Company
rowleycompany.com

Glue Basting Tips
Purple Daisies Quilting
purpledaisiesquilting.com

Shears and Serrated Scissors
KAI Scissors
kaiscissors.com

Multipurpose Cloth
Roc-lon Multipurpose Cloth
Dick Blick Art Materials
dickblick.com

Zippers
Zipit
etsy.com/shop/zipit

Want even more creative content?

Make it,
snap it,
share it
using
#ctpublishing